HOLISTIC
POWERNASIUM
BEYOND SCHOOL

Kevin Hajin Choi

Vine & Branch

HOLISTIC POWERNASIUM BEYOND SCHOOL
Copyright © 2024 by Kevin Hajin Choi
Published by Tree & Branch
All rights reserved. First printed in August 2024 in South Korea.
Unless otherwise indicated, Bible quotations aer taken from the *New International Version*.
Cover Design: Hanhee Kim
Content Design and Chief Editor: David Nah
Editors: Sarah Pahl, Kennah McCurry
ISBN: 978-11-91366-04-4-03230

CONTENTS

"While doing joint research with All Nations School, I was impressed at how the heightening expectations on educational achievements did not increase the burden on the students. The students are always vibrant with their wide smiles, joy, consistent participation in the positive influence that they will assert on the world, and a distinct sense of anticipation."

- Keith Walters (Professor, California Baptist University)

People who have 'Something Different' can navigate through their lives with confidence and without comparing themselves to others. Those who have 'Something Different' become 'Somebody Different'. Rather than just being 'No. 1', they become the 'Only 1'- someone who lives life a bit differently and unlike any other. Whether it may be education in the household or at school, the purpose of education is in creating such people. Alas, what is the reality of our education? Aren't we driving our children into a mad dash towards the sole goal of becoming 'No. 1'?

My point is: 'education is the Alpha and Omega of life'. It is the duty of our schools to provide education that empowers our children to overcome inferiority complexes, loneliness, evil, closed mindedness, and to maximize intellectual ability and break through their limits. However, there are no schools around us that fulfill this duty- none that are fit to be the 'model school'. Whether it may be a public school, private school, alternative school, or an academy, there simply aren't any schools that can merge and renew the value of education.

I built a school in a region of North East Asia with my disciples about 20 years ago, envisioning a school that gives laughter and empowerment to our children. Above all else, we put all our efforts into raising the 'power' of our students. We dare say that the education system in place today is one that the Jewish people (who are well known for their thorough education) would envy. "How can you be so certain?"- one may ask. The state of a tree can be seen through its fruit. As previously seen from the letter of the dean of academic affairs of an American university, our 'fruit' are astonishingly healthy and outstanding. Many students from Korean schools undergo an uneven education and display excellent scholastic performance but poor emotional stability, or vice versa. Graduates of All Nations School show stellar academic results as well as outstanding emotional stability. If this is not the fruit of proper education, what is? Now, I will introduce Holistic Powernasium Beyond School, the core of our education system, to all those interested in education such as students, parents, teachers, and administrators. I deeply hope that this book will be the tool that opens new realms of education.

Power Base

———

Building
the Powernasium

———

01

Building
the Powernasium

"Stay hungry, stay foolish."

This was Steve Job's closing statement for his commencement speech at Stanford University. Although we frequently emphasize the mindset of 'staying hungry', we rarely tell people to 'stay foolish'. However, it only takes a moment of observation to realize that it is the fools who make history.

My Brief Testimony

I, too, once lived life striving for success. In that life, I tried so hard to become rich. I was twenty-eight years old with a PhD from KAIST and was working as a researcher at Daedeok Science Complex, Korea. I mimicked my senior colleague and collected expensive, luxury home audio systems, and elegantly learnt golf during my weekdays. There was more. On weekends, I travelled everywhere that had a good review and was as busy as a bee enjoying my life to its fullest. Then one day, as I was returning home after another glorious day, a sudden uneasiness crept up inside me.

"Is it REALLY okay to live like this?"

By day, I was a polite, intellectual scientist. By night, I was but a pitiful soul wandering through the night streets, swept off my feet by waves of entertainment. I was heading towards death, and however glamorous or happy my life seemed during each fleeting moment, everything would eventually end with nothing- nothing but 'death'. That was it. My life wasn't striding towards success; it was a flight from the constant fear of failure. I thought I had fame and honor, but in the end, all I saw was myself being chased by loneliness and fear.

I had a Doctoral degree in engineering from KAIST and a Postdoctoral fellowship from Stanford University. It would have been easy for me to acquire a comfortable life. However, now that I had looked into the depths of my life, there was no way that I could settle for a life that was only striving for success. I was filled with a life mission to help those who were lost in the midst of 'survival', 'successes', and 'craving', just like myself in the past, and to help them find and fulfill a dream and hope that was rooted in the right values. In the end, I rejected offers that many would die for, was called a mad man by those who knew me and headed to my mission field.

The situation in that country 26 years ago was not what it is now. The economy would remain closed for many more years, and the country was isolated both socially and culturally. It was a backward country with financial problems and no guarantee of safety or human rights. My friends were rightfully concerned for me.

Once I arrived in my mission field, I interacted with young students while working as a university professor, and rather than simply teaching them how to be successful in academia, I worked hard to help them find the true purpose of life and the right motivation for study. I guided them to study, not out of desire for personal success, but for the vision of exerting a greater and beneficial influence on the world. Although a professor's salary at the time was less than 100 dollars, I spent several thousands of dollars every month to meet, teach, and serve my students. While some may question why the expenses were so high, the college students I was helping were far from the college students we generally imagine. These students tasted orange juice and jam for the very first time when they visited my house. They lived in a tiny country home where their entire family lived in a single room. They were so poor that they had to wear nylon socks in the coldest winter. Offering them a pair of my own socks and providing them with clothes and food was a big part of my service.

I had initially planned to serve for 3 years, which was equivalent to the years of military service I had been exempted from. (All young people in Korea should go to the army as Korea is divided into the capitalist South Korea and the communist North Korea, and they are hostile to each other.) However, as I watched my college students gradually transform through education, I could only imagine how much more effective it would be if children were properly educated from an even younger age. From that day forward, my vocation became a 'School Planter'- a creator of schools!

A School is Planted

Dreams and visions materialize when you share them with others. One day, I told my students that I wanted to build a school. In other words, I had shared my vision with them. What was amazing, however, was that my students immediately responded that they would like to join me. So, that was how a total to twelve fools consisting of a university professor, teachers, businessmen, salary men, students studying in the US and a few others came together. What could be impossible if not just one, but a crowd of people were determined to risk their lives for a cause?

First off, we decided to name the school 'All Nations School'(All nations are called Wanbang in Chinese and Manbang in Korean) to make multicultural global servant leaders who serve all nations in the world through education and through the love of God. We then planted the school flag in an empty field that we saw near Hope City. Based on my experience in real estate investment back in Korea, I was able to see the development potential in this barren land which was yet to have any roads or electricity. In a few decades, it would become a land too expensive to even dream of purchasing. As predicted, the government of Hope City had purchased the right to use the land and was just about to open it up for businesses or schools, and we were their first customers. The person in charge may have been touched by the burning passion and determination in our eyes because we were able to buy the school grounds at an extremely affordable price.

A vast cornfield with snow. We put the flag in, walked around and prayed.

Alas, it wasn't easy to get the building permit. We had to get stamps from 33 departments to get the final permit and it was common practice to bribe through each step. However, I could not build a school for the proper education of young children through dishonest methods. So, we decided to be fools once again. We did the only thing that we could and visited the officials repeatedly. If once wasn't enough, twice.

If twice wasn't enough, we went three times. We visited them again, and again, and again, and again, and after such painstaking efforts, we were finally able to collect all 33 stamps. I cannot imagine what would have happened had we caved into reality and followed the unrighteous method. All Nations School's honesty, that is deemed highly reliable today, is the result of upholding honesty relentlessly without giving up.

Just like that, starting with the establishment of our middle school in 2003, we went on to build a high school, a kindergarten, an elementary school, a cafeteria, a gymnasium, a leadership center, and more buildings, one at a time. We didn't start this because we had a lot of money. Our assets, if any, were our shared dream and vision.

02

More than a School, a Powernasium

Why do we educate our children? Have you ever wondered why you educate your child? We can find a hint in 2 Timothy 3:16-17.

"All Scripture is God-breathed and is useful for teaching, rebuking, correcting and training in righteousness, so that the servant of God may be thoroughly equipped for every good work." (2 Timothy 3:16-17)

This verse clearly indicates the purpose of education. Education thoroughly equips servants of God for every good work. In other words, it empowers. We need to raise individuals who aren't just good at studying or just religious but who have developed various strengths and a deep faith like the Bible characters, Joseph, Joshua, David,

Daniel, and so on.

What Does It Mean 'To Educate'?

"To educate means to nurture a person in both intellect and character." Most people would nod in agreement upon hearing this statement. It is obvious that a person's character and intellect need to be trained together. However, something seems to be missing. Why do we feel so stuck in darkness? What is the point of having a well-formed character and intellect if we are unable to utilize them? This is the reason why we need 'power'.

"To educate means to empower a person so that they may assert influence."

Education isn't to raise 'grades' but to raise 'abilities.' Studying isn't the simple acquisition of knowledge, but the development of various powers:

First, Network Power, a.k.a. the ability to communicate and form relationships. Children feel happy when their 'relationships' such as teacher-student relationships, friendships, and parent-child relationships are properly established. If they have Network Power, they are able to maintain a happy life within their family, school, and society.

"A new command I give you: Love one another. As I have loved you, so you must love one another." (John 13:34)

Second, Mental Power. Mental stability and having a challenging mindset are extremely important in creating a successful life.

"Be strong and very courageous. Be careful to obey all the law my servant Moses gave you; do not turn from it to the right or to the left, that you may be successful wherever you go." (Joshua 1:7)

Third, Brain Power. Students should be empowered to develop their strengths in critical thinking and self-expression. They should overflow with creativity rather than study based on rote memorization.

"[Wisdom] is more precious than rubies; nothing you desire can compare with her." (Proverbs 3:15)

Fourth, Moral Power. Our future society will place importance on the process as well as on achievement; thus, higher moral strength is necessary to become a leader respected by society. True competitive edge comes from moral power.

"Blessed is the one who does not walk in step with the wicked or stand in the way that sinners take or sit in the company of mockers, but whose delight is in the law of the Lord, and who meditates on His law day and night." (Psalms 1:1-2)

Fifth, Leadership Power. People living in the 21st century need to be multicultural, equipped with a global perspective, and servant leadership skills. Our children must begin with self-leadership, develop it into a leadership that benefits the community, and eventually mature to become a global leader who influences societies, countries, and the entire world.

"Sitting down, Jesus called the Twelve and said, 'Anyone who wants to be first must be the very last, and the servant of all.'" (Mark 9:35)

Sixth, Body Power. Eating and exercising greatly influences the brain. Love for junk food leads to a 'junk life'. Disliking exercise prevents us from even thinking about a productive life.

"Dear friend, I pray that you may enjoy good health and that all may go well with you, even as your soul is getting along well." (3 John 1:2)

Seventh, Spiritual Power. We become powerful when we stop focusing only on material things, and instead, start looking at our lives as a whole and taking on the quest to live a meaningful and valuable life.

"Therefore, I urge you, brothers and sisters, in view of God's mercy, to offer your bodies as a living sacrifice, holy and pleasing to God—this is your true and proper worship." (Romans 12:1)

A person who is equipped with these seven powers equally is more than prepared to become a happy, competent individual who is capable of exerting good influences.

More Than a School, 'Powernasium'

In Germany, 'Gymnasium' refers to a secondary educational system that prepares students for college. If we look into the roots of the word, 'Gym' means physical exercise and activities and 'Nasium' means a place for increasing strength through training. The word itself is derived from the Greek word 'Gymnasion' which was a place that functioned as a training facility as well as a place for the intellectual pursuits of young adults. This word was split into two parts, hereby becoming a training facility (gym) in English-speaking countries and an educational facility in German speaking-countries. On the other hand, words such as 學校(Xuexio in Chinese) and school only represent educational institutions in a very narrow sense as they only mean 'a place where students learn cognitively'. In that sense, we could say that the German expression for educational institutions is more appropriate. However, I see the need to take it a step further. Schools should become a 'Powernasium'- a place where students are trained and nurtured to strengthen and enhance their holistic power.

"The Powernasium is a holistic power plant where talented individuals train their various powers to make a better influence!"

Schools and parents should enhance the seven distinct powers within the students, and the students themselves should be able to maximize their strength within the Powernasium. In the following chapters, I will explain the "how to" of how each power can be trained and introduce some of our incredible results. As you continue through each page of this book, you will be able to see the complete roadmap that leads to superpowered leaders of the 21st century.

A German Gymnasium

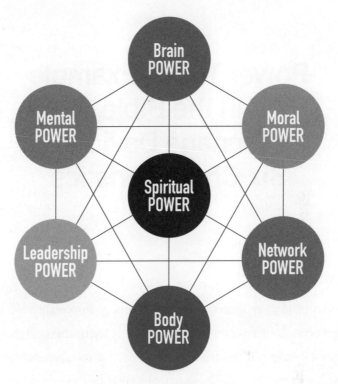

The Powernasium Curriculum

03

Power Talent Example in the Bible, Teenage David's Six Characteristics

Recommendation letters play an extremely important role in the hiring process for a new employee. Likewise, David, a biblical character, saw his life take a dramatic turn because of a recommendation. Let me introduce the six characteristics of David that are mentioned in 1 Samuel 16:18. One of King Saul's servants recommends David by describing him as follows.

"One of the servants answered, 'I have seen a son of Jesse of Bethlehem who knows how to play the harp. He is a brave man and a warrior. He speaks well and is a fine-looking man. And the LORD is with him.'" (1 Samuel 16:18)

The recommender describes David by mentioning six things: his harp skills, bravery, warriorship, eloquence of speech, fine looking appearance, and the fact that the Lord is with him. I want to call this David's 'sixpack' because these six characteristics are packed into a single package and recommended to the king. Do you know how old David was at this time? Since David had defeated Goliath before he turned twenty, we can assume that he was in his late teens. In modern times, he would have been a student in high school and in the prime of his teenage years.

1. He Plays the Harp

David cured King Saul's illness by playing the harp whenever he was mentally unstable. Perhaps, David could have been the first musical therapist in history. His natural talent in music allowed him to enter the palace where he met and became close friends with the king's son, Jonathan.

How can we reinterpret his harp skills to fit the present day? It can be seen as the utilization of special skills or talents. Parents should help their children so that they may develop their talents to the fullest. God wants us to maximize the talents that He has given us whether it may be in singing, playing an instrument, or drawing. Therefore, we emphasize the following message to our students.

"Society no longer asks for intellectual ability only. Having talent is a strength. Discover your talent - your God-given gift and maximize it."

2. He is Brave

David took care of his father's flock and often came across lions and bears that stole his sheep. However, David never gave up on his sheep. He chased them to the very end, fought with the lion or bear, and brought back the sheep. As such, David attended to his duty with passion and responsibility and was an active and tenacious person.

There are wild animals that are attacking your child. A lion called low grades, a bear called personal relations, a wolf called sense of inferiority, and a fox called highly addictive games. We need to fight and win against them no matter what. Shouldn't parents focus on nurturing their children to become brave leaders who can fight against all these beasts and rise to victory? This generation absolutely requires leaders who will march onwards with passion and confidence.

3. He is a Warrior

The fight between David and Goliath is one of the most famous fights in the world. Back in those days, the choice weapon for battle was a sword and shield. However, David chose a method that only he had honed - the sling method. Don't underestimate the sling. We can calculate its force using the circular motion equation of physics.

$V = 2 \times 3.14NR$

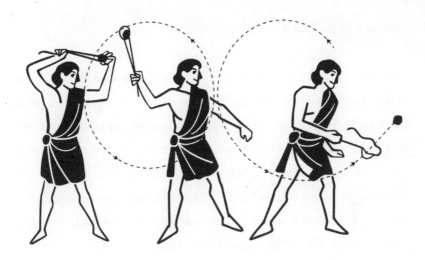

V is the speed at which the sling was released, N is the number of rotations per second, and R is the radius of the sphere that is created when the sling is slung, which is equivalent to the length of the arm and the sling. If we estimate that David rotates the sling 4~5 times per second and that the radius is 1 meter, the speed at which David releases the stone from the sling is approximately 90 ~113km/hr. Thus, we can see that the sling was a secret weapon that could shoot as fast as a baseball pitcher. David's accuracy was also unquestionable since it was honed to a sniper-level through the numerous battles with beasts. If you still feel doubtful, read the Bible verse below which mentions that there was a sling-shot troop before David.

"Among all these soldiers there were seven hundred select troops who were left-handed, each of whom could sling a stone at a hair and not miss." (Judges 20:16)

Clearly God had trained David from a young age for the fight with Goliath. In a modern sense, the sling can be interpreted as an outstanding personal specialty. We have to hone our own slings. We should never follow the trend being followed by the rest of the world. We need to build our own personal strengths. What is the sling that you will place into your child's hand? That will become their one and only personal strength that will help them win the world, which is why they should become the 'Only 1' rather than 'No.1'.

4. He Speaks Well

The phrase 'he speaks well' doesn't simply mean that he was a good speaker - it means that he knew how to express his thoughts eloquently as well as how to communicate and persuade. David was a master of persuasion. How do we know this? Think about it: the future of the whole country depended on the fight with Goliath, but in reality, David was a mere candle standing before a storm named Goliath. David had visited the war fronts to bring lunch to his brothers when he discovered his people cowering under Goliath's vigor. David wasn't a soldier; he was more of a beast fighter. Was it realistic for the Israelites to wholeheartedly welcome this lad who didn't have any actual battle experience and send him off to fight Goliath? It was just plain crazy to leave the fate of the country in his hands. The situation is even comedic;

it is as if an ant is standing on top of an elephant and proclaiming that it will 'trample this beast to death'.

However, David begins to persuade King Saul.

"You shouldn't lose heart. I will go out and fight. I fought with numerous lions and bears while tending my flock and I have won every single time. I retrieved all the sheep that they stole from me. God has saved me. Likewise, the God who has saved me countless times will most definitely raise my hand in victory in the fight against that Philistine."

David explained his strengths, strong conviction, and his experiences of God's helping hand with determined resolution. In the end, King Saul changed his mind and decided to send David to battle.

Our children also need such persuasion, not for the fulfillment of their own desires but for God's Kingdom. This is why they need to have good faith and read a lot of books. All Nations School has a 'three-minute speech' training session. Students choose a topic and work in small groups to research and discuss the topic and prepare a short essay for presentation. Society is searching for people who are good at communication who can think, create a line of reasoning, and write about it, talented individuals who have the skills to persuade those drenched in a victim mentality.

5. He is a Fine-looking Man

In English, the question 'How are you?' is replied with 'I'm fine'. This answer shouldn't just be words but should also be written on the person's face. As such, 'fine-looking' refers to a fine impression rather than a beautiful physical appearance. Thus, he was 'fine-looking' even from a distance.

If there is something that is more important than a 'pretty face', it is a fine impression and a fine expression. However beautiful one's face may be, it would not be able to bring joy to others if it is constantly covered with a worrisome and gloomy expression. If I were a CEO who was selecting new employees to hire, I would most definitely look at the potential candidate's expressions. A person who brings excitement and a happy air to those around them can bring a huge benefit to the company. It would uplift the community that they belong to.

We need to throw away any pessimistic mindset, cringey expression, or cold look. Instead, we should equip our children with an expression that brightens the atmosphere and a 'fine-looking' face.

6. The Lord is With Him

Experiencing God's presence from a young age is a huge asset in life. These people have high self-esteem and are confident in all aspects. In other words, they are bold rather than hesitant or shy. What is impossible and where in the world is it impossible to go when we are with the Lord almighty? We are able to run towards the goal and challenge the impossible because we have a clear purpose in life. Therefore, children need a special 'catchphrase of faith' during their teenage years.

How many songs of Psalms has David written? Each of those songs praise the Lord who has been with David. Psalms 23, which touches the hearts of many people is also a song that David wrote while tending his sheep as a teenager. This is the reason why our children have to experience our God who is our shepherd.

"The Lord is my shepherd, I lack nothing.

He makes me lie down in green pastures, He leads me beside quiet waters, He refreshes my soul.

He guides me along the right paths for His name's sake.

Even though I walk through the darkest valley,

I will fear no evil, for You are with me.

Your rod and Your staff, they comfort me.

You prepare a table before me in the presence of my enemies.

You anoint my head with oil, my cup overflows.

Surely Your goodness and love will follow me all the days of my life, and I will dwell in the house of the Lord forever."

Teenage David was a talented leader who had been evenly equipped with faith (spiritual power), creativity and a specialty (brain power), optimism and passion (mental power), communication skills (network power), great physical strength (body power), patriotism (moral power), and sheep-raising skills (leadership power). He is exactly what the current society and companies look for. No organization desires a person who has good faith but lacks skill. We basically learned from David that we should not separate faith and skill. It is awful to imagine a Christian who compromises and surrenders and stoops below the world called Goliath.

A Student, Isaac's Psalms 23

Isaac is currently an eighth grader. He says that he is deeply experiencing God's love every day at All Nations School. God trained Isaac through his life here. As a result, he came to fully realize how weak he was, and each time, he depended and leaned on the huge tree that is God. Isaac found himself always reaching out to God as he continued to pray and communicate with Him. Just like David, Isaac wrote 'Isaac's Psalms 23' to praise God and shared it with his fellow students.

"The Lord is my huge tree; I will never leave there.
I will lie upon Him and rest in His shade.
He sprouts a new bud in a bed of rotten grass that is my heart.
He pours water onto my thirsty heart.

Even though I shed a tear at night and

yearn for home in a dark room in a foreign land,

I will fear no evil,

for my lips can call to You and my heart longs for You.

You wipe my tears with a cloth of love.

Even when I hate myself because of my sins and arrogance,

You stand by me as a gardener and correct my crooked branches.

I will follow You, call Your name, and entrust myself to the Lord forever."

Power One

NETWORK POWER

POWERNASIUM
POWERNASIUM
POWERNASIUM
POWERNASIUM
POWERNASIUM
POWERNASIUM
POWERNASIUM

01

More than a School,
We are a Family

We all live within the boundaries of our culture. Therefore, we cannot transform a country's education by only changing the educational system. We have to change the culture that governs our way of thinking, which is not an easy task. From the beginning, we tried hard to implement a new school culture. We replaced profanity with kind language, competition with cooperation, rote memorization with discussion, authoritarian relationships with family-like relationships, and top-down relationships with mentor-mentee relationships. We encouraged students to study, not for their own success, but so that each student may become a pathway of blessings for thousands more. Above all else, we paid particular attention to the relationship between peers since that was the most important element for a happy school experience. Thankfully, our efforts paid off in the form of a unique culture.

All Nations School's Unique Culture:
- We don't have any hierarchical structure of senior-junior which is especially strong in Korean and Japanese culture. There are many cases in which seniors try to intimidate juniors.
- Our school is cell-phone free. Korean students are very addicted to smartphones and online games because of their very fast internet speeds.
- All teachers know the names of all students. They should call the students' names to enhance their intimacy.
- The principal's office is near the students. It is not a large, authoritative office, but a space where students can easily communicate with the principal,

Abolishment of the Senior-Junior Hierarchy

"You don't have to use honorifics for me."

"Really? That is not common for Koreans."

"Yes, you can abandon those habits from Korea. Here at our school, you can just call me brother, alright?" (Koreans usually do not call the name of someone else.)

"Okay. senior, no, I mean, brother!"

In Korea, the authoritarian relationship between senior and junior students is even worse than between teachers and students. People even joke that the senior-junior hierarchy among teenagers is even scarier than what you would find in the military. Juniors cannot say a single word even if their seniors use physical or verbal violence against them. If a junior lives in a dormitory, the authority and oppression he faces becomes unbearable. Sometimes they are ordered to secretly purchase alcohol and cigarettes. No wonder school life is miserable. Thus, we decided from the very beginning that our school will abolish such hierarchical culture, and therefore we do the following:

- We do not have titles such as senior or junior.
- We only have sisters and brothers just as in a family.
- Most families do not use honorifics between brothers and sisters, so neither do our students.
- Students do not verbally or physically abuse their peers or order them around just because of their age difference.
- Students form a mentor-mentee relationship.

Freshmen are astounded by our unique culture. They feel grateful for the senior students who approach them to show them around school and who take the initiative to serve them and set a good example.

"More Than a School, We Are a Family!"

A Student's Testimony about
'No Senior-Junior' Culture

Hachang is a student who studied in a boarding school full of hierarchy for two years before transferring to our school. After experiencing the 'No Senior-Junior' culture which is a 180 degree change from his experience in Korea, he described the joy he felt as something he would only feel on Paradise Planet.

"Hello, my name is Hachang. At the previous school I attended prior to coming to this school, seniors barely came to school and teachers didn't care. When I went back to my dorm every day, older students made me do many difficult errands because I was the youngest among the residents. The easiest task was to cook 5 ramens and deliver them to the senior students. I then had to wait until they were done so that I could do the dishes too. I hated the weekend above all else. There were no school meals on weekends, so I had to get up even earlier.

When I moved to All Nations School, the older students took care of the younger students first, did not order errands, and did not curse. Also, teachers would ask me what was wrong and offer me consultation if I seemed even slightly down. Also, if I asked my teachers just one question, they would kindly teach me so much more. I love my school more than any other school because the younger students are loved by the older students and because our teachers are awesome. It's like heaven.

I'm in the middle of my first semester now. Previously, it was hard for me to speak even a sentence without cursing or using profane words; but here in this school, I naturally began to speak kinder words because I feel self-conscious when using bad language.

Although I had undergone so many changes, I also faced barriers that seemed unsolvable. The issue? Friendship. I had a hard time becoming friends with my peers, and we even fought and eventually fell apart to a point where we wouldn't even talk to each other. As time passed by, I started to pray with tears and tried as the older students and teachers guided me to do because I thought that this situation wasn't okay. As a result, I was able to break through the wall of friendship. I now have close friends, talk a lot, and have many friends with whom I feel good even when we share a glance. Whenever I see my friends, I feel so thankful to the older students and teachers who helped me form these relationships. I want to grow up to become like my seniors and become an older brother who gives good advice and ample love to those younger than me."

Ask your child, your student, or yourself this question: "Are you happy at school?" How would a student be able to enjoy studying if they aren't happy in their peer or senior-junior relationships? Network Power begins when we accept this problem and correct it.

School upgrades into another form of family through the 'No Senior-Junior' culture.

What Does SNS Mean?
It Means School Network Service.

Nowadays, most students focus on smartphones without exercising or having hobbies. Especially, SNS(Social Network Service) has gained immense popularity since the introduction of smartphones. Heartful face-to-face conversations have disappeared and the urge to stay connected to something has resulted in the booming success of SNS companies. Thanks to SNS, companies have earned huge profits while students have made huge losses in their time. However, what students really need is not a social network, but a school network. Schools need to be able to provide their students with a School Network Service. How are students supposed to apply Network Power when they cannot communicate and form relationships with those whom they spend most of their day? Students need to develop a face-to-face and heart-to-heart Network Power.

We have banned the possession of smartphones within school premises in order to help our students build Network Power. Almost every student cringes upon hearing this policy and yells "Oh My God!". On the other hand, parents react with a beaming smile on their faces. Give it a week, and the effect becomes apparent. The reason why students think that they cannot go without their smartphones is quite simple: it's because everyone else has it. They feel peer-pressure and fear the situation of being the only person without a cell phone. That's why we flipped matters around to solve the problem. If everybody 'doesn't have' it, then the norm would be to 'not have' it. In fact, any student who brings their phone will become the cheeky cheater and the foul player who broke the rules. Let's look at the transformation undergone by our children who used to sigh as if giving up their phones meant the end of the world.

"I wondered how I would survive without my phone, but now I feel more comfortable without it."

"At first, I didn't know what to do with my fingers. Now my fingers feel more secure around a pen."

"I could hear hallucinations of my phone's vibrations. Well, it's gone now."

"I grew closer to my friends now that I don't use my cell phone. I have more fun talking with my friends during each break."

"I have a lot of spare time now that I don't have a smartphone. I use that time to read instead. I can feel my knowledge deepening."

Whenever I introduce this school policy, people question whether it was possible for us only because we are a boarding school. They worry that students will get sucked right back into their smartphones the moment they leave school. Of course, that is a legitimate point. However, the effect will be sufficient if we are able to create a smartphone-free environment, even if it may be limited to school premises. If you are not a boarding school, try collecting your children's' smartphones during school hours or even during a set schedule in the household. You will receive a strong initial pushback and lots of complaints about discomfort, but the positive result will continue to increase over time.

The Principal's Office as a Cafe

What do the students think of the principal? Is the principal seen as someone too difficult to approach? There is an idiom that says, 'out of sight, out of mind'. What would happen if students fell far from the sight of the principal? The principal may become more interested in the school's performance results rather than in the students. Their focus may shift to nagging the teachers to get more students into Ivy League universities. Therefore, we decided to reestablish the principal-student relationship:

- Locate the principal's office in front of the classrooms.
- Have a one-on-one advising session with every single new student.
- Everyone including the principal should memorize the details of all the students.
- Turn the principal's office into a cafe so that students may come by freely at break times.

In most schools, the principal's office and classrooms tend to be far apart. That is why we brought the principal's office closer to the students. Now the chattering and laughter of the students float into the principal's office like sweet music. Also, now that the students are more 'in sight', they are more 'in mind'. Principal Hyun says that she finds herself missing the chattering of her students whenever she is on a business trip.

There was something that worried Principal Hyun. Although the principal's office was closer to the students, the students were still distant from the principal. How could she become closer to the students? That was when she thought of the milk cafe. First, she purchased a fridge for the principal's office. Then, she stocked it up with milk and some simple snacks. She planned so that the principal's office would be free to visit for any student who wanted to drink milk. With time, students who had initially found it difficult to approach the principal's office began to drop by frequently as if the place was their own home. The idea was a big success.

Don't think of the students as if they are wasting your precious time. It will only be a ten-minute break. Business can wait. We utilize these ten minutes very efficiently. We talk with the children while they feast on milk and snacks. The conversation topic varies from student to student. The students used to drop by for the milk, but now they come to talk with their principal. While it could be difficult for students to visit the principal's office just with their troubles and questions, they are able to drop by more comfortably now that they can drop by "for milk and snacks".

Students having a conversation with the principal over a cup of milk in the principal's office.

One Day Dorm Parent

Teachers are the core of school education. Teachers are more than just people who teach in a classroom. They need to demonstrate leadership to students and parents. However, this leadership comes from dedication. We need teachers to teach by showing their lives. What authority would a teacher's words have if teachers went around catching students who smoke and drink while they themselves enjoyed their alcohol and cigarettes? Instead of wasting time grumbling about the downfall of the authority of educators, we need to spend that time to connect with one more student.

Our teachers take turns to be 'one-day dorm parents'. This movement was intended to bring the teachers a step closer to their students. The following story is the experience of one of our teachers, Miss Sally Cho, as a one-day dorm parent.

"One of the important tasks of teachers at All Nations School is taking on the role of dorm parent. The personalities that students display when you meet them in their dormitories is drastically different from what they would show in the classrooms. The students feel freer and more comfortable in their dorms because it is a second home to them.

It is a fun experience because you get to see a different side of your students and because you get to build a closer relationship with them. Also, it's a good opportunity to see their overall lifestyles.

I still remember the time when I was a dorm parent during my first semester at this school. I was patrolling as usual when I saw the lights on in one of the rooms. When I entered the room, I saw vomit on the floor and a student (the room leader) cleaning it up quietly with a composed expression. I asked the room leader about the situation.

"What happened?"

"We were sleeping after roll call because it was time to sleep when a younger student on the top bunk suddenly threw up on the floor. I was sleeping on the bed in the bottom, but it happened so suddenly...."

I tried to help clean up the mess, but the room leader insisted that she would complete the task by herself since she had already started. So I directed my attention to the sick student, giving her medicine and keeping her warm. However, the student began to throw up once again. I became concerned about the severity of the student's condition, so I brought the student to the dorm parent's room and laid her on the bed. The best I could do was to pray for her. Thankfully, the student slept well through the night, although she occasionally moved around in her sleep.

I waited for the night to pass. When morning came, I hurried the student over to the school nurse. It turned out to be a bad upset stomach. Later, the student opened her heart to me and followed me well. I'm very happy because the student likes me and trusts me quite a lot, quite possibly due to the incident that night."

You can't be as relaxed as when you are at home while you are acting as the dorm parent. There are so many things that need to be checked carefully, including whether there are any sick students, if there is anything that needs to be repaired, whether the students are self-studying properly, and whether the relationships between roommates are alright. I find myself completely worn out after a long night of dorm parent duties checking for sick students, managing the closing and opening time of entrances, and making sure that all students are out for their morning exercise routine.

However, the dorm parent system provides teachers with a valuable platform to communicate with the students and a time to learn how to love them. Sometimes, we get to understand the hearts of parents. Above all else, the greatest value lies in the fact we are given a heart to pray for our students because we get to know the students thoroughly. I have learnt so many things while working as the dorm parent. Also, students seem to feel more comfortable around teachers when we are dorm parents."

The miracles of the All Nations School began from self-sacrificing teachers like Miss Sally Cho. Students who join our school achieve higher grades and enter prestigious universities. They also show a change in character and attitude. What could have caused these miracles? The root of our secret lies in our devoted and talented teachers. Power isn't made through teaching but through love. It is our firm and unchanged educational philosophy that love is the energy source of power.

02

Like the Shepherd of a Flock

How can schools provide a school network service? What can we do to help students develop their network power in school? We decided to reestablish the teacher-student relationship. We decided to memorize the names of dozens of new students who are welcomed each year. The principles of attitude of teachers to students are:

- All teachers memorize the names of all the new students beforehand
  (ALL students, and not just students in their own class).
- Teachers memorize individual details as well as the names of the students through the personal details report.
- Teachers spend time together to share the name, picture, and other specifics of each new student.
- Teachers do not use words such as 'You there' or 'Oi' that may

seem impersonal or distant.

- Teachers approach the students first and call their names.
- Teachers take special care of students who are ill.

Imagine that a teacher whom you've met for the very first time calls you by your name. Your heart will open, and you will see the teacher in a different light. You will feel intimate with them. A student will have a hard time studying if they do not like their teacher. Thus, teachers and students must maintain a close relationship above all else. For this, the teacher must approach the students first.

Teachers Taking Tests

My college student, Dr. Han Kim, joined our school immediately after he received his doctorate from Louisville, Kentucky, U.S.A. As a vice-principal of our school, he gathers all the teachers to conduct a new student identification test before a new student begins school. The following is an extract from an interview taken by a press company that was deeply interested in our method.

"We heard that the teachers and students at All Nations School have a deep, family-like relationship."

"Yes. Parents and new students have to write details including the student's strengths and weaknesses, topics of study, visions, goals, health issues, hobbies, and family background when they apply to our school. Teachers thoroughly read and analyze the contents of the applications."

"It wouldn't be easy to memorize the details of so many students. What's your secret?"

"We print the name and picture of each student beforehand and tape it on our desks. That way, we can memorize their names and faces every day. You can memorize quickly once you understand the trait of each student."

"It seems like education begins with the memorization of the names of each student."

"Yes. The objective of this task is to take interest in each individual student. We also hold a meeting in which we look at the name and picture of the new student, analyze their problems, and discuss the direction and methodology we should implement to educate them based on the contents of their applications."

"You even hold a meeting?"

"Of course. The following steps become much easier if you put in your efforts at the beginning."

When the time comes for the student to begin school, we undergo a final check up to welcome them. A few days prior to their arrival, teachers have to take a student analysis test that is far more difficult than any college entrance exam. Questions include how the students came to our school, their year of birth, what they aspire to be, food that they like and dislike, allergies (if any), peer relationships, and family environment. Solving each problem leads to the overall analysis of the student's situation. Then, when we call the new student by their name, the student gasps and asks, "How do you know my name?" We laugh and reply, "We know the name of your parents too!"

It is said that 'to teach is to touch a life forever'. You need to open the hearts of your students in order to open their ears. While some may think of this as a tiresome task, the effects are tenfold. Think of the students who are ridden by all kinds of stress. Establishing a happy learning environment for the students comes before the tiredness of teachers.

Creating a Cell Group Called Ranch.

Imagine scenery with a pasture, a ranch, a shepherd, and a flock. There is a passage in the Bible that says:

"The good shepherd lays down his life for the sheep" (John 10:11)

If the school is pasture, then who would be the shepherd? It would be none other than the teachers. The flock? That would be the students, of course. Aside from the traditional grades and classes, we also have a grouping system called Ranch where students of different classes and grades are intermingled. Teachers in charge of grades or classes are called 'class teachers', and teachers in charge of Ranches are called 'shepherds'. Class teachers direct their students in matters regarding academics, and shepherds focus on touching the hearts of their students.

Ranch gatherings happen once a week and members can dine out if they need to. There's also an event that members absolutely enjoy, and that is to sleep over at the shepherd's house. On that day, the shepherd teachers prepare and feed their students with all kinds of delicious menus. Afterwards, the group makes the dishes together and plays games. Basically, they enjoy a pajama night. The shepherd and sheep talk through the night.

A Teacher's Testimony About Pajama Night

"When the new semester starts and I meet new ranch students, everyone runs towards me. Spaghetti, garlic bread, tiramisu, galbi... Et cetera. The students who list all the foods they want to eat are adorable. I know all too well how much students are waiting and looking forward to that time. A night out at my house where we eat together, and everyone sits around and watches a movie together in their pajamas and spends the night together is a special day that makes us feel that the teacher and the students have become one family.

From spending days shopping to prepare food for fifteen or so people, to preparing snacks for pajama nights, the preparations for the ranch students are enormous. The carefully prepared food disappears in the blink of an eye. When I see everyone with their mouths full of food and happy that it tastes like their moms ate at home, I smile happily too.

Then everyone sits around and shares their first impressions, or compliments their friends' good behaviors, and shares these honest thoughts that they couldn't share in the hustle and bustle of school. Thinking that this heartwarming moment will make the children smile fondly when they think of their school days in the distant future, they smile again, saying, "Happy girls!"

My students wake up early the next morning and gather at the table for breakfast, rubbing their eyes that can't open properly. Even those things look so pretty; it makes me feel like their mom.

I pray my students to grow up to be people who will expand the scope of their family and serve the people around them and their families."

Dinner at a Ranch teacher's house

Pajama night at the shepherd teacher's house

A Place of Sharing, the Ranch

Ranches have different names. Kenya, Myanmar, Kazakhstan.... We decided to name Ranch after countries with hopes to naturally bring children to have global perspectives. Ranch members are told to research the country which their Ranch is named after.

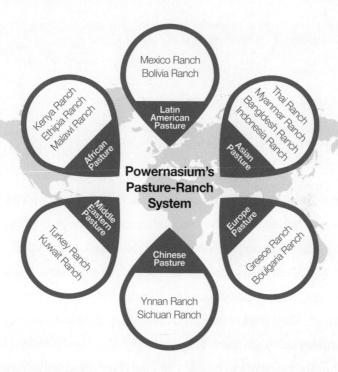

Powernasium's Pasture-Ranch System

Mexico Ranch
Bolivia Ranch
Latin American Pasture

Kenya Ranch
Ethiopia Ranch
Malawi Ranch
African Pasture

Thai Ranch
Myanmar Ranch
Bangldesh Ranch
Indonesia Ranch
Asian Pasture

Middle Eastern Pasture
Turkey Ranch
Kuwait Ranch

Europe Pasture
Greece Ranch
Boulgaria Ranch

Chinese Pasture
Ynnan Ranch
Sichuan Ranch

Ranches are reorganized each semester. Each Ranch has two 'shepherd' teachers and one 'supporting shepherd'. A few Ranches collectively form a 'pasture', and each pasture has a 'pasture keeper' teacher. The pasture keeper looks after the shepherds, and the shepherds look after the sheep. Supporting shepherds are usually students who are selected based on how well they take care of their peers and how caring they are because the supporting shepherd is a position of complete service and no ordering authority. Ranch gatherings occur in the following order as an example.

10 minutes	Share about the past week
30 minutes	Share about weekly topics
5 minutes	Wrap up & move to dining area inside/outside school
30~50 minutes	Have dinner together & fellowship

There are so many benefits to the Ranch system. Above all else, it deepens the relationship between students and teachers. People cannot live by cognitive ability alone. Everyone feels loneliness. Everyone craves love. Everyone wants to communicate. Sure, there is importance in having a wide circle of personal connections, but everyone wants a true friend. They want to give and receive help from friends. They want to be counseled by teachers. They want to make changes in their habits. Ranch is the place where all this can take place effectively. It's a place where people can get together without being burdened by academics and a place where they can find the vision which motivates them to study. It is a place where they can find a clear purpose of life and a goal for their education.

Furthermore, shepherd teachers meticulously document the life, emotions, and topics of consultation for each of their students. Then they upload the information on the teacher's intranet so that any teacher may view the documents if necessary. This forms a 'spiderweb network' through which every teacher can help each individual student more effectively.

There is a saying that 'students learn what they see'. Students live alongside their teachers through the Ranch system, whereby the students get to learn from the lives of their own teachers beyond all else. This 'lesson through life' is the most certain method through which our students are transformed.

Ranch Becomes Family.

Students find the Ranch system very refreshing because they had never experienced anything like it. In a Ranch, the shepherd supports the children in all aspects of their lives such as their overall lives, emotions, and relationship with their parents rather than just focusing on their studies. Particularly, new students are able to make friends and adjust to their new, foreign environment through the Ranch gatherings. With time, they become so close to their shepherd teachers as to even call them mom and dad. I asked a question to these children. 'What does Ranch mean to you?'

"As a student who had joined last semester, I adjusted to the school much more quickly, felt loads of love from my teachers, and learnt so many more lessons [thanks to our Ranch]. The Ranch system is a platform to share love and joy and is necessary."

"It brings us together and allows us to accept each other as a family. It can also promote the development of character."

"It allows us to communicate."

"It brings us together and we are able to share our lives with our friends and teachers through our Ranches."

"It is a healthy family in which we learn, fight (sometimes), and grow together."

The word 'family' recurred among the students the most. So, what does the expansion of the scope of 'family' mean? It means that there are that many people whom they love. This is the origin of network power. Bullying and isolating cultures naturally disintegrated as the Ranch becomes a family. There are teachers at school who are responsible for a class and many others who are not. Wouldn't we be able to catch all three birds- intellect, character, and personal relations- if these remaining teachers took care of a Ranch?

03

Relationships
Training

What is the most difficult thing about your career? If you think that you will be full of happiness if you just work hard and get a job, you are very mistaken. Because as soon as you get a job, scary monsters are waiting for you. It is 'human relations.' A few years ago, <Business on Communication>, which has about 1 million office workers as members, investigated the causes of unhappiness in the workplace. As a result, 'interpersonal relationships at work are difficult' accounted for the highest proportion at 47%. When asked why they were happy at work, on the other hand, 41% of employees answered 'maintaining good interpersonal relationships at work.' Additionally, 29% responded that they 'recognize their abilities.' 'Salary' accounted for 20%, and 'appropriate hiring' accounted for 8%. As such, office workers believe that relationships, rather than skills or salary at work, have the greatest impact on happiness.

Meanwhile, what are the biggest concerns of Korean teenagers? According to a survey by the Ministry of Gender Equality and Family, as shown in the statistics below, the most common difficulties were 'interpersonal relationships', followed by 'study and occupation', 'deviance and delinquency', and 'personality'. Despite this situation, schools do not even think about making efforts or developing systems for human relationships. Parents are also focusing only on their children's college admission qualifications. This is what we are missing in the educational environment. At our school, students are able to experience a 'difference in culture' in the classrooms and a 'difference in personality' in the dormitories because we have students who have lived in Korea, Chinese-speaking countries, and English-speaking countries.

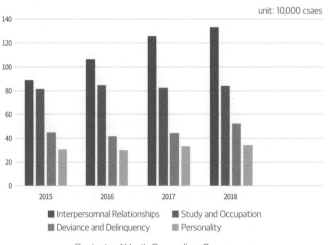

Contents of Youth Counseling. Source:
Korea Youth Counseling and Welfare Development Institute

What does it mean to 'making human relationships? Let's look at this extract from 'Everyone Communicates, Few Connect' written by John Maxwell, the author of an international bestseller and a Best Writer selected by New York Times and Wall Street Journal.

"Relationship Ing is never about me. It is about the person I communicate with.

Likewise, when you try to make a relationship, it is not about you. It is about your opponent. You must overcome yourself first. Change your focus from the inside out, and from yourself to others."

Voila. Changing your perspective! Our youth are becoming increasingly inexperienced in making relationships. This is the result of feeding self-centeredness and a strong ego that makes people think only of themselves. People are too busy to look out for other people. We need to train to change our perspectives before it is too late. Good grades and diplomas from top universities aren't the only keys to success. It is those who have strong personal relationship skills who become leaders and achieve successful lives. Do you want to direct your children to have successful lives? Do you want to raise them to become leaders? If that is the case, I urge all parents, schools, and students to start training in human relationships.

Is there a way to nurture network power within our schools and homes? The answer is again in community training. Have up to five children share a single room for 1~2 weeks and allow them to bustle and live together. Recreational events or seminars don't help much. Instead, develop educational programs with activities that students can enjoy with their roommates and presentations that students get to prepare and present themselves. A better method would be to have the children live together at school. They need to be given time to bump into each other.

Dorms, The Best Place for Relationship Training

Private schools must provide for their own financial needs since they do not receive any funding from the government; but that also means that they are subject to less intervention. They are supported so that they may operate as autonomically as possible. That is how we were able to develop a creative educational program for our school. In this country, all schools are mandated to have a dormitory. We decided to use this mandatory dorm as a training platform- a place to raise community network power.

One may imagine a dorm room that houses one to two students. However, that is too few to establish sufficient training. Thus, we created a few rules:

- We do not have single or double rooms, which promotes individualism.
- 4~6 students will share a room and live as a community.
- Members of each room shall include: a new student, junior student,

senior student, and a room leader; this will assist the swift adaptation of the new student.

- Each room member will keep a personal plant for increased affinity with nature.
- An Open House will be held each year, and each room will decide their own theme, whereby honing their creativity and cooperation.
- The room leader is a position to serve the younger students and not one of ordering authority.
- A floor leader and vice-leader will be assigned to each floor so that they may raise responsibility and servant leadership.
- Teachers shall take turns to be the one-day dorm parents to enter into the lives of students.

"I used to have the role of maintaining the girl's dormitory and checking the rooms every morning and evening, and I always helped the students summarize their tasks and made sure that everyone was in their dorms. So, I was only able to go to sleep after making sure that everyone else was asleep. I also checked whether all the girls were present at the daily morning exercise at 6.30am in the morning, and it was a valuable experience through which I got to know the other students even better.

I was sharing the same room with three 7th grade students who needed a lot of love and attention. Their parents had either passed away or were abroad for a very long time to earn money. That may have been the reason why these girls were always filled with negative thoughts. I helped them to think more positively and taught them how beautiful life was. Soon we became a family that understood each other.

One day, I accidentally overheard some students talking badly about me behind my back. I felt so distressed, and I cried so much once I returned to my room after school. That was the first time that I ever showed my weakness to anyone else. The 7th grade girls blotted my tears with a handkerchief. As they wiped away my tears, I was overwhelmed with immense strength. My roommates continued to say nothing and brought a basin of water to wash my feet for me. More tears welled up. I remembered the words that I had previously told them. Have courage. There's nothing you won't be able to endure. All these hardships will turn into steppingstones for you. That's right. The words that I had once said had become words that I now needed.

Through that period, I was able to look back at the way I worked and was able to accept what I had done wrong. Afterwards, I tried hard to treat my friends with a caring and serving heart. I want to continue to share my love and become as a bridge for acts of loving help."

That was the story of Hailey, a dorm leader student. Hailey went on to study abroad in the United States after graduating All Nations School, and she returned to us after graduating college in 2013. Our students are greatly motivated whenever they see her talking freely in three different languages. Hailey's experience became a cornerstone for our school dormitory policies when we were going through various trial and errors just after the establishment of the school ten years ago.

Let's listen to the story of another student, Chaerin.

"A dorm is a place like home full of love. Above all, the dorm is the most suitable place to refine relationships. The reason why I define the view of living in this way is because I have personally felt and experienced that it is a place of value and change.

It is no exaggeration to say that the real transformation of the students begins with the dormitory, which has two floors and more than 50 people live on one floor. As such, we need to treat public items more carefully and use them sparingly. So, if you listen to the roll call of our dormitory, you can see that more than half of them are suggestions for the use of dormitories. "Please take your laundry on time," "Please close the gate," and "Please don't make noise during nap hours." In this way, we learn something called "caring" in our lives. It's amazing to see my friends and younger siblings, who came to the room without knocking when they first came to the room, borrowed clothes, and left them without saying thank you, and didn't clean up themselves, but they took the initiative to learn and be considerate.

These things may seem small and insignificant, but when these habits accumulate every day and become a part of our daily lives, we can see great results. As the habit accumulates, my consideration, warmth, and goodness grow together, and when I graduate from school, I will be able to proudly smell the fragrance of the 'consideration' in my heart, which no one has ever learned. I am convinced that the 'consideration' that I learned at school will be a valuable help and asset for us to live in the world.

If so, is our dormitory a problem-free place where you are always considerate? Absolutely not. I would like to describe the dorm as 'a valley where angular stones come together and collide to make them round and soft'. It's a place where people with so many different personalities, different family backgrounds, and people who grew up in different regions come together, so there are more problems and conflicts. I was no exception. When I was a freshman, I was so timid and selfish. But the dorm didn't let me think about it like this. Through my friends around the dorm, I was able to understand other people's personalities and learn that I needed to change. And I also slowly began to learn how to communicate my intentions clearly, which is necessary in society.

Now, as a room leader, I have grown enough to lead my younger friends and serve them warmly. If we think of ourselves as stones, we have a lot of potholes and sharp points. As these ugly and sharp stones tumble against each other, we sometimes feel pain and sadness, but when we reach the end of the valley, we realize that another piece has healed from a new dent that we don't know about, and that the sharp place has become soft and round.

The students were not considerate from the beginning. There was a time when they were selfish, outspoken, blunt, and sensitive, and they struggled with a lot of friction and worries. However, in the view of living in a world where everything from one's attitude to one's own corners is revealed, one experiences a change as one breaks oneself. With the help of my friends, I realize my own inadequacies and take the first step to go out into the world and reach out to others through understanding others."

What thoughts came to your mind as you read this student's writing? How mature she is! Do not dismiss adolescence as a time of turmoil. Adolescence is like a springtime in life. As long as they go through this period well, their dreams will grow, and their personality will be perfected.

Most people feel the difficulties of interpersonal relationships only when they become professionals, but it is often too late to develop the power to overcome those things, only to fall into trouble and consider themselves unhappy. They don't know how to behave because they lack understanding of human beings, so they try to avoid them first. But imagine developing networking skills in adolescence. We have a habit of putting off important things because we are not in a hurry. Laying the foundations during adolescence will make college and social life much easier.

We do not live alone in this world. You have to learn to live together. We need to build network power first at home and at school. The more this power increases, the more enjoyable school life and happy social life will be possible.

Power Two

MENTAL
POWER

01

Students need
Detox

When we think of Moses, we immediately picture a man who stands before the parting sea and a leader who guides the Israelites across the Red Sea and through the wilderness. It gives me the chills when I imagine the Red Sea splitting apart. However, Moses was an ordinary man just like you and me. After he ran away from the palace and after forty years of an utterly ordinary life, Moses came across a great turning point in his life in the year that he turned eighty.

While he was tending his flock just like any other day, Moses came across a bush that didn't burn up though it was on fire. Upon this peculiar sight Moses said to himself,

"I will turn aside and see."

As he approached the bush, Moses heard a fearful and majestic voice. It was a holy voice that he had never heard before.

"Moses! Moses! Take off your sandals, for the place where you are standing is holy ground."

From this point onwards, Moses' life was transformed into a life with God. God didn't force Moses to take on His mission. Instead, God first took 'detox' steps in order to remove the toxins- or 'tox'- from him.

We can see what toxes Moses had when we look at the conversation between God and Moses in Exodus chapters 3 and 4. Let's analyze the five toxes that were in Moses by observing how he reacted to God's given mission.

Moses' Five Toxes

We would be viewing the Bible very fragmentarily if we jumped to the conclusion that these were Moses' five excuses. Since words are the expressions of a person's heart and the heart is a reflection on a person's character, we need to think about Moses' entire life to understand his answers.

Moses had lived forty years as a prince and then another forty years as a shepherd. What would these eighty years of his life have been like? We need to picture his life and peer into the 'tox that are piled up in Moses' heart' that are hidden in his words. The word 'tox' refers to all negative factors that can influence the health, growth, personality, and strengths of a person's body, soul, and mind. While some may call these 'internal wounds', I prefer the term 'tox' rather than 'wound'.

Now, let's jump into the conversation between God and Moses to look at each of Moses' tox.

Moses' first answer has the following implication.

"I know what I am. I don't deserve it and I don't have what it takes to do it."

Thus, Moses' self-esteem was lower than ever. Moses had gone from being a prince of high status to being a fugitive overnight and he practically became a homeless man once he ran away from Egypt to Midian. Then one day, he saved Zipporah and her sisters from some bullies. Through this event, he married Zipporah and became the son-in-law of Jethro (also known as Reuel) who was a priest of Midian. Let's assume that Moses went from being a prince to homeless, homeless to a commoner, then a commoner to someone with a bit more status thanks to his father-in-law but was still only reminiscing about his glorious past and stuck in a life without a clear vision. How bleak would his existence seem in comparison?

Let's find the tox that is hidden in his second reply.

"Okay. Let's say that I went. People would ask me the name of the person who sent me, but I don't know much about You. You said that

You'll be with me, but…so what?"

Moses' second tox was his lack of faith in God. Moses didn't know much about God, and he didn't have the heart to trust Him. Moses was the son-in-law of a Midian priest, a priest of foreign people. This means that Moss had watched his father-in-law's idolatry from a proximity and was even benefiting from it. Therefore, it would be illogical to claim that Moses was completely uninfluenced by it.

The Midian people worshipped an idol called Baal. The Canaanites also had various names for their idols including Baal, Asherah, and Ashtoreth. What about Egypt, where Moses resided throughout his youth? Moses had lived in a culture that was filled with countless idols including Apis, the golden calf that symbolizes power and abundance, so this would have been the cultural background from which he was questioning God. At that moment, God replied.

"I am who I am."

This is the background based on which we call God 'Jehovah' or 'Yahweh' in the Old Testament. Thus, Jehovah means 'He who is who He is' who is everlasting and unchanging. God provided Moses with an extensive answer in Exodus 3:14~22 and explained, persuaded, and prophesized so that Moses could trust Him.

Let's look at the third reply.

"God appeared to you? Ha! Even a passing dog would laugh at you. Aren't you a fugitive? Yet do you still claim that we should listen to you? Don't you even dare."

Moses was afraid that people were bound to react like this. He was stuck in his experience when he had become an outcast and he was so stricken with a victim mentality that he could not even dream of exerting leadership. Well, he had been ostracized by both the royal family of Egypt as well as his own people. As such, Moses was ruled by the painful memories of his past. However, God knew very well of what was going on in Moses' mind and showed him two undeniable miracles in Exodus 4:2~9 to show him that He was God.

"If I can use a mere staff, can I not use you?"

God showed the miracle through the staff to pass on this message to Moses, and then made Moses' hand leprous and clean again whereby giving him an unbelievable experience. As such, God planted certainty in Moses and encouraged him. Here, we can see how God doesn't give up when He is giving courage and calling His people. This would be a great time for Moses to say, "I have finally realized that I won't be the one doing it. It will be You, God, and You will be by my side. Use me as Your tool." However, Moses continues to give more frustrating answers. The fourth tox went like this.

"I am bad with words because my mouth is slow, and my tongue is stiff. You need to be multi-talented in all kinds of fields to be a leader.... so I don't think I can do it."

At this point, God might have wanted to flick Moses on the forehead. If you are a teacher, you come across so many children who are like this- children who don't think about their own strengths, only focus on what others are good at, and fall into an inferiority complex. Their underlying thoughts are pessimistic. God speaks to Moses to transform such thoughts into positive ones, but Moses talks back to God one last time.

"Oh, I don't know. It's not going to be me anyways so look for someone else."

How frustrating. God finally shows His anger after having kept His cool throughout the conversation. The Bible expresses it as, 'The anger of the Lord was burned against Moses.' How angry must God have been for His anger to become burning flames? If I were God, I might have said, "Oh, you unworthy child. How can you still not understand after I've told you all that? Never mind, then. Do you think I've got no one else? Oh, you fool."

However, God yields a step. "Alright, alright. You know what a great speaker your brother Aaron is, right? I will guide Aaron's mouth as well as yours."

Perhaps 'fear of doing things alone' may have been the final tox that was packed inside Moses. God gave courage to Moses by giving him Aaron as a coworker.

Moses had eighty years-worth of tox piled up inside him. So, God first began to detox the tox in his spirit and the tox in his heart. God restored his self-esteem, brought him to gain trust in the Lord, planted a sense of mission, and transformed the evasion of responsibility that arose from fear and inferiority complex into courage.

Moses' Five Toxes

Our students are no different from Moses. Do you want your children to live a more confident, happy, wonderful, and valuable life? The answer is simple. Detox the tox in the heart. We need to guide our students through each step of the detox process with patience the way God had detoxed Moses. That way, they can be prepared for God's use.

A+ Student, Poly's Tox and Her Empowering Through Detox

Poly was incredibly good at studying and almost always had a grade of 100. She said:

"I extremely care about my grades and fear exams. Isn't my identity the scores and grades that are written in my high school transcript? I feel unhappy when I don't receive a 100 because I failed to get a 100 and I feel unhappy when I do receive a 100 because I feel pressured to get a 100 again the next time. When will I ever be happy?"

Why does she become obsessed with her grades? Poly believed that the judging criteria for students was their grades. What would you do for her? We diagnosed her state of mind, and we could see that she had an affinity for grades, inferiority, and fear from perfectionism. We first needed to plant a proper worldview to bring forth a change in perspective. She finally came to make this testimony through the efforts of her teachers and lectures on world outlook.

"According to the Bible, I am a precious being who has been uniquely created by God and thus should live a life of helping others who are precious like me. However, according to the world's perspective of survival of the fittest, I am but a creature born by chance. I need to compete to survive in this fierce world and to enjoy what the world has to offer. This perspective makes the world a cold and dark space."

We had to help her undergo spiritual and mental detox simultaneously. As we went ahead with the detox process to remove these tox, we helped her change her perspective on studying and set aside some time to rethink the purpose and vision of studying. Then we held a counseling session a month later.

We approached Poly and gave her the following advice.

"Here's a homework assignment for you, Poly. We want you to play this week. Also, try to be lenient to yourself even if your weekly test results are lower than usual, alright?"

This was our advice to help her break free from her obsession with grades. Then, after a month of detoxing and a second counseling session, Poly confessed:

"I used to care so much about studying because I thought that getting good grades was my only strength. Many people believe that only visible blessings such as in studying, art, music, and sports are gifts that matter. However, God gave us a greater power that cannot be seen- for example, the ability to understand people's hearts and to love- as a gift. God created each of us equally and uniquely and prepared for each of us a special plan. These days, I've stopped studying for grades and have begun to search for the vision for my teenage years. I still don't have a clear idea of what I should do. However, I do QT or read in the morning instead of studying for exams now that I am more peaceful in my heart. I've started studying something new too, and that is the 'happy study' of growing as a member, server, and a leader of the community and as a human being."

Can studying become a happy task? The greed for scores, the greed for grades, the greed for acceptance to a prestigious university.... These 'greeds 'are what cause the disputes between parents and their children and the competition and fights among friends.

"The greedy stir up conflict, but those who trust in the Lord will prosper." (Proverb 28:25)

So, what is the secret to happy studying? Poly emphasized:

"I've let go of my scores but haven't let go of my learning heart and diligent work!"

What a wonderful realization! Poly's heart was filled with peace.

Happy studying has begun. She had received the keys to the happy study room and the secret to entering this secret room was to 'let go of the scores'. There's more: the peace that God gives us when we diligently attend to our studies makes all barricades of obsessions, anxiety, and nervousness clear out like fog from the study paths in our brains.

"Great peace have those who love your law, and nothing can make them stumble." (Psalms 119:165)

Like the changes of Moses and Poly, detoxing our spirit and mind doesn't end there- it empowers us and gives us powers to exert great influences on oneself and others.

02

Strengthening Mental Power through Gratitude

There are things that are consistently trying to make the students slip and fall. Those things are pessimistic thinking, comparative mindset, inferiority, timidness, and perfectionism that stop the students from taking on challenges. We need to transform pessimistic thinking into positive thinking, free the students from comparative mindsets so they may truly see how special they are and help them to build muscle so that they may take on challenges and push through.

Have you ever thought about what makes the basics of mental power? The answer is a positive mindset. How can we become positive people? Through over ten years of research, we discovered that there is a magic potion that can turn even the most pessimistic person into a positive person. That magic potion is 'gratitude' emphasized in Christianity.

"Be joyful always; pray continually; give thanks in all circumstances, for this is God's will for you in Christ Jesus."(1 Thessalonians 5:16~18)

The church has emphasized gratitude, but weirdly enough, its importance hasn't been recognized much in schools. It's probably because they weren't aware of the power of gratitude. Let me introduce the effectiveness of 'gratitude' in transforming a person to have a positive mindset as well as a gratitude program that we are implementing at our school.

The Science of Gratitude

Professor Robert Emmons, who is known as the pioneer of gratitude science, of UC Davis and Professor Michael McCullough of Miami University conducted a joint research project on 192 college students to study the effect of gratitude. Participating students were randomly divided into three groups and were required to write down once a week. What they recorded was as follows. (see J. Personality and Social Psychology, 84, no2, 377-389, 2003)

Gratitude Group - This group was asked to focus solely on being thankful. They recorded five reasons for thankfulness, such as 'I am thankful for my understanding friends.'

Hassles Group - This group was asked to record five things that angered or frustrated them, such as, 'I had hard time because there were no parking spots available.'

Events Group - This group was asked to record five neutral things disregarding any concept of giving thanks or complaint, such as 'I cleaned my room'.

The experiment was conducted over ten weeks. As a result, the Gratitude Group showed the highest improvement in the quality of life, better health, and approximately 40 minutes more exercise time than the other groups. They also developed a more optimistic disposition.

Then they conducted a second experiment. The participants were divided into groups of Gratitude, Hassles, and Comparison because the underlying theory was that people experienced happiness when they felt superiority from comparing themselves to others. This time, participants were asked to record every day for two weeks. Although it was difficult to detect any changes in health since the experiment was performed over a short period of time, they could observe that the positive effect increased as the frequency of gratitude increased. Thus, they discovered that the happiness that comes from gratitude is far greater than the happiness that comes from comparing ourselves to other people. Furthermore, they discovered that the participants in the Gratitude Group had the highest sociability.

They decided to conduct a third experiment. This time, they recruited 65 adults who were chronic patients with neuromuscular disabilities instead of healthy and young students. These participants felt pain in their joints and muscles and experienced difficulties going through everyday life. These people had a big reason to be unsatisfied with their lives. Just as in the previous experiment, the participants were divided into groups, Gratitude Group and Regular Group, and were asked to record for a period of three weeks. Again, the Gratitude Group displayed a higher level of satisfaction in life, higher optimism about the future, and 30 more minutes of sleep as well as a better quality of sleep (Good quality of sleep for patients is an important criterion of overall quality of life. In general, people who sleep well tend to be healthier and happier than those who don't. The finding here was that people could still be happier despite being in a difficult and tough environment if they formed a habit of gratitude. That was the moment when it was scientifically proven that happiness came from gratitude rather than from conditions.

Gratitude and School Life

Could the effectiveness of gratitude be expanded to encompass even children and adolescents? Professor Jeffrey Froh conducted Professor Robert Emmons' experiment on teenagers. First, he conducted an experiment on the effect of gratitude on 221 middle school students. (see J. School Psychology, 46, 213-233, 2008) He divided the students from 11 classes into three random groups and performed the experiment designed by Emmons and McCullough for two weeks. As a result, students who kept a gratitude journal displayed the highest level of satisfaction and positivity. Additionally, Professor Froh conducted a study with his fellow researchers on 1,035 high school students between the ages of 14 to 19. Students who kept a gratitude journal scaled higher grades, higher satisfaction in life, higher sociability, lower jealousy, and lower depression. Recent studies have also published results as shown in the picture below that reveal the effect of gratitude on a student's school life. In the picture, the numerical value distinguishes how direct an effect gratitude has on each category. Thankful students experience a higher satisfaction in life as well as in their relationships with parents, teachers, and friends, along with a greater possibility to achieve higher grades.

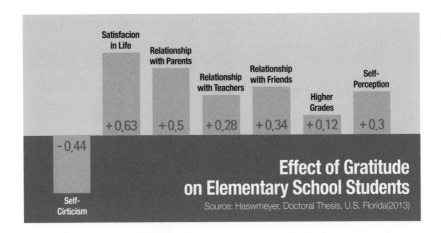

They also discovered that writing letters of thanks has an immense positive effect. Students between the ages 8~19 were divided into two groups (Gratitude and Daily Life). The Gratitude Group was told to think of a person to whom they hadn't sufficiently expressed their gratitude to, write a letter of thanks, then to go and read it to that person, and finally to write down what they felt. The Daily Life Group was told to write down their activities from the previous day and what they felt. This experiment was repeated every day for two weeks. Through numerous experiments on the effects of gratitude, it was revealed that thankful students received 10% less stress than students who weren't. In other words, they had developed a higher tolerance to stress and a 10% higher resilience. That's not all. Thankful students received 20% more A's than the control group and were 13% less violent. In the case of working adults, research shows that thankful people are happier than those who aren't and receive a 6% higher salary on average.

What do you think? Shouldn't we allow our children to first enjoy the benefits of gratitude prior to being stressed out about college entrance exams? There is no better exercise when raising your children to become successful individuals than training them to be thankful. It should become second nature. However, there is a limit to the amount of such training that a person can do on their own because the resistance and repulsion that is already ingrained in their minds drives them to give up. That is why our school organized the 'Thank You Project' which is participated in by the entire student body for 21 days. The project goes as follows.

- List five things that you are thankful for every day and contemplate it.
- Write a gratitude journal entry every day.
- Share topics of thanks with your roommates every night (3~5 minutes).

- Set up a Tree of Thanks on each floor of the dorm and attach notes on what you are grateful for.

Reshaping From the Inside Out Through Gratitude

Kyle joined All Nations School last year. I was dumbfounded when I read the book reviews that he submitted for the required reading prior to matriculation. Let me share a few of his reviews.

"I was a bit discontented when I was told to read these books and write book reviews. I thought they were trying to turn the books into bestsellers by using the students."

"In the end, the documentary on the lowest-class people of India aims to increase audience ratings through the flamboyant language of the writer."

We observed that Kyle was a boy whose heart was filled with a negative and complaining attitude. People had to exist for his sake and his perspective of the world was very crooked. We felt the need to turn his negative mindset into a positive one by 'giving thanks training' which is known as the best way of detox. It was the most needed training for Kyle who said something negative every time he opened his mouth. One day, after over a year of detoxing efforts, he shared the following confession.

"I am thankful that I can play the piano and that my talents can be used for someone else whether it may be a difficult or easy song. Even though I could have impressed people on my own and although I am now in a hidden position, I am thankful that I can be a part of the music and that people can find the right tune through me and make a beautiful harmony."

Finally, Kyle was able to realize who he was and what a community was. Furthermore, his pessimistic attitude to life was corrected and he was transformed into a positive and thankful student.

Gratitude and Academic Achievement

Let's introduce another student named Hoon. He was a student who showed a selfish tendency in community life and used profanity in every other sentence. His grades weren't bad, usually ranging from C+ to B, but the results fluctuated with every test. The gratitude activity sometimes has an incredible effect on such students. It triggers change in their attitude, which in turn transforms their relationships with friends along with their study attitude. So, we started the gratitude activity hoping for such positive effects. The following graph reflects Hoon's test result data.

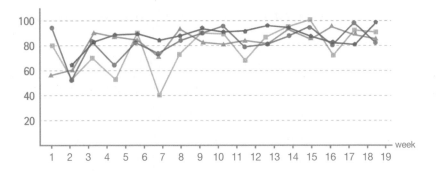

We created this graph to document the change in Hoon's results in the weekly tests. As shown in this picture, Hoon's grades display less fluctuation and a gradual increase from the C~B range to the B~A range. Most students who participate in the gratitude activity tend to show higher consistency in their grades. That means that they are more emotionally stabilized. According to our experience, students tend to show better academic results after an average of 3 months of gratitude activity. The gratitude activity improves their emotions, character, and sociability, thus also having a very positive impact on their academics.

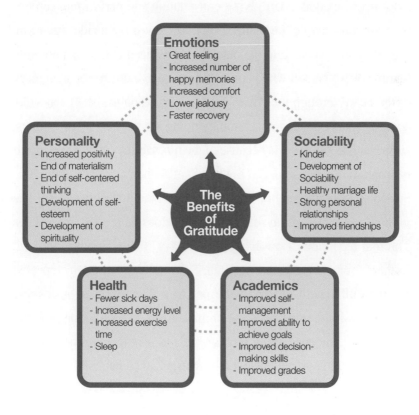

Building Mental Power
Through the Habit of Gratitude

Maxwell Maltz, the author of ' The new Psycho-Cybernetics', was a cosmetic surgeon. After giving consultation and performing surgery on numerous people, he realized that correcting the inside was more important than correcting the outside. He realized that it was possible to transform a person who is distorted inside by performing a 'surgery of the heart' through the '21-day rule'. According to the 21-day rule, anything can be made into a habit by doing it consistently for 21 days. How is this possible? It is because of the moldability of the brain called neuroplasticity. A person can finally change when a positive thought is passed on from the cerebral cortex and imprinted in the brain stem. The minimum number of days that is required for this process is 21 days. Through repetition of positivity for 21 days, a new circuit is formed, further strengthened, and resistance is reduced through repeated practice, ultimately changing the person's disposition to a positive one. A pessimist turns into an optimist. Are you wondering whether this 'internal surgery' really works? Let's look at the common factors shared between our students who have established habits of gratitude.

- They are passionate about their studies.
- Their faces are light and lively.
- They are optimistic and active.
- They transform their weaknesses into strengths.

- They have high self-confidence which enables them to break through difficulties with ease.
- They maintain good personal relationships.
- They do not get stressed easily.
- They are full of hopeful energy and leadership skills.

"Why won't you study?", "Studying is for your own benefit.", "We'd be so ashamed if you failed to get into a good university." …

Why don't we train them in gratitude before dumping all this stress upon them? Let's build their mental power through the power of gratitude. It will improve their studies as well as their relationships with their friends, teachers, and family.

03

The Power
to Break Through

The following are a few traits of students who excel in language studies.

- They imitate actively.
- They chatter regardless of whether they may be right or wrong.
- They aren't shy and are always active.
- They express themselves with their action even if their knowledge of the foreign language is limited.

Do you know where these traits come from? They come from incredible mental power, the courage to 'just give it a shot'.

The David Project for Mental Training

Let's take a look at the Bible person David again. A war erupted between Israel and Philistine while David was still a young shepherd, and Goliath, a Philistine general and a giant who terrorized the Israelite soldiers with his enormous physique, was taunting the Israelites by cursing Israel and their God and by daring them to fight him one on one if anyone had the guts to do so. David, who had come to visit his brothers, went to the king upon seeing the Israelite soldiers frozen in fear. This youth less than 20 years old then voiced his will to fight.

"Let no one lose heart on account of this Philistine."

By this he meant that losing courage was losing the battle without even a fight. Although the king initially refused to send him to the war front because he didn't want to waste a young man's life and bright future, he was eventually taken by David's persistent persuasion. David refused the armor that was too big for him as well as the heavy sword and selected five smooth stones for his sling instead. Can you imagine the look on Goliath's face when he saw David come before him? However, there was something that Goliath the giant did not know about: David was actually a well experienced fighter who had fought against numerous beasts to protect his sheep.

This is the mental power that students need most. The education in many countries is raising all their children to be cowards. Children are driven to study under the fear and severe pressure of getting that college acceptance and job. Our children must learn how to study proactively. Only then will they be able to naturally acquire independence and self-directed learning.

David Project #1,
A Long-Distance Walking Trip

Many parents just want their children to live in safety rather than challenge. When a child is about to give it a go, they are told, "It's too dangerous", "You'll get hurt", or "Study if you have the time to do that", and finally are stopped en route. With spoons feeding them, hands carrying their bags to school for them, homework being done for them, and classes being registered for them, children are constantly stopped from taking on a challenge. Every day of our lives is a continuum of challenges. For how long do you plan to keep your child in the 'safety' of your lap? The first thing that parents need to do to raise their children's mental power is to stop requiring them to be perfect and to let them just give it a shot.

Our school holds a walking trip every spring. It is an event where we select a course beforehand to walk all day long. We walk about 20~25 kilometers once we begin to walk. At 8:00am, all the students and teachers gather at the school gates and gather into smaller teams. Each class carries a flag and bravely begins the trip. Members chat, laugh, joke around, and have a lively time. Then two hours later, a few students become visibly tired. Five hours later, silence. Everybody is too busy focusing their energy on completing the trek. It takes about seven hours to walk back to school. After this event, you can easily spot students who are wobbling around school with blistered feet or sore muscles. "What is the purpose of having this boot camp-like walking trip at school?", you may ask. There are many benefits to this walking trip:

- Relationships between classmates are improved.
- Friendships are deepened as students help each other out.
- Students and teachers get a chance to talk a lot, leading to closer relationships and consultations.
- Close, family-like ties are made.
- They experience the great feeling of accomplishment.

Just like how you need muscles to maintain a healthy lifestyle, you need mental muscles for your mind. I go weight training and walking whenever I get the chance. Exercises include bench press, leg press, low pull, pull down, squats, and lunges. For each exercise, there is a certain weight that I can lift, pull, or push. However, I always go 5% higher than my limit. That is to increase the limit of my muscular strength. After a month or two, I can see my limit increasing from a 'barely-90kg' to an 'easy-100kg'. As such, we need to steadily improve our muscle strength. This also goes for the muscle strength of the mind. Let's design challenges in various fields and challenge our children. The outcome of such challenges? Satisfaction of accomplishment.

This will directly affect their studies too. Children will host more and more positive thoughts to giving it a go. Why aren't our child's grades improving? Why does our child get cranky whenever I tell them to start studying? If these are some of your concerns, then what your child needs is mental power. Make challenge programs in fields aside from academics to raise the mental power of your children.

"My eyes opened an hour earlier than usual. And seeing the other students already bustling around, I thought that I should get started too. I got to the basketball court and saw all the students and teachers (except the 9th graders) already prepared and ready to go. The teacher made a few important announcements and we soon marched through the front gates like a group of ants going to gather food.

Soon, we walked by a dusty construction site. I was very fascinated since I had never seen such a large field of construction. Several tens of apartments were being built simultaneously, and it was really amazing to see.

Instead of focusing on the ache in my legs, I thought about what I would do during the remaining five-ish hours of expedition, not counting the distance we had already walked up to this point. After wondering, 'What should I do?', I went to talk with our Ranch teacher, David. Since I wanted to study in the U.S., I thought that this would be a good chance to chat and learn more about the country. David may have been wanting someone to talk to too, because he answered my questions and more. He told me about American food, universities, families, cultures, and even promised that he would pick me up at the airport if I ever visited. It felt as if I was already on a plane to the United States. Around that time, we sat with our groups to have a light meal. I drooled when I saw the other group next to us take out rice balls: all I had was a cream bun because I hadn't had the chance to prepare any rice. At that moment, our teacher took out some rice and eggs and mixed those simple ingredients with some sesame oil and soy sauce to make egg-rice! The egg-rice tasted like an oasis in the middle of the desert and the sesame oil: soy sauce ratio was absolute perfection. We were once again filled with energy after we emptied the bowl through an aggressive (and not at all peaceful) spoon-combat. It was a really fun brunch time.

The remaining time passed smoothly like a river. We arrived at our destination much quicker than the last time. I was grateful that we had completed the trip safely with nobody hurt and that I got to know more about our teacher David (who I wasn't that close to before) as well as about the United States. Above all else, I felt proud and thankful that we had completed this trip as a united group. The weather was awesome and it was a time to remember. This walking trip brought all the students and teachers together through a single event. This truly is an asset and a valuable tradition of our school. I can't wait for the next trip!"

Walking Trip. We walk 20~25 kilometers every spring.

David Project #2
Boot Camp

Let's look at the daily routine of an average, modern-day student. They barely wake up to the sharp voice of their mom, have half a breakfast, and then scamper off to school after yelling that they are late. It's the mom's job to clean up their rooms, and all that the child is left to do is to study at school, study at an after-school cram school, finish their homework, finish cram school homework, play internet games, go on SNS, and sleep. What leader can be raised from such a lifestyle? In other words, mental training has been long gone. It is difficult to find any form of training for standing alone or overcoming problems. It is those who have high mental power that succeed in society. Thus, schools should also adopt mental training.

We have a training session that all new students must undergo upon arrival. It is called 'boot camp'. We invite instructors from outside the school. So sometimes we call it basic military training. The following is the translated version of a writing submitted by Chen after he finished this training.

"Finally. I completed the group training camp that begins upon matriculation. Until now, I had never lived as a community before. However, all students must live in the dorm and must study, eat, sleep, and even snack within the school premises. The new student 'mental training camp' welcomed me on the day that I arrived. Four men wearing a serious expression and military outerwear stood before us. They gave us a brief welcome and began a close-order drill. We were divided into groups of ten whereby each group formed a squad. The instructors demonstrated how to stand in a single row and how to turn right, left, and back. Then we gathered into squads to receive training from a designated instructor.

I had never experienced such an atmosphere before. I was always used to doing whatever I wanted, but now I had to form a single line with other people and every mistake on my part affected everyone in my squad. Although we had initially begun the training with a light heart, we had no choice but to get a grip of ourselves as time passed by. We walked and walked, ran and ran...It was also the first time that I had sweat so much.

There were times that I was breathing so hard and times that I really wanted to give up, but I just clenched my teeth and pushed through because I didn't want to cause my teammates to have a disadvantage.

Freshmen's boot camp

It really felt as if we were in the army rather than at school. Although I knew none of my squad members, we naturally started talking to each other within a single day and we grew so close so fast out of the simple fact that we were in this together. We didn't even have our mobile phones, and this allowed me to feel a freedom that I hadn't experienced before.

Six of us stayed in the same dorm room. We didn't have a

shower in each room, which meant that we had to use a communal shower, washroom, and loo. We had to prepare our own toiletries such as shampoo and soap since those weren't communal items. Each squad had 10 minutes to shower. The spray water from the shower booth was so refreshing. I washed every part of my sweat-drenched body. Rest time had never felt this meaningful throughout my entire life. After the shower, I returned to the dorm and flopped on my bed. The saying was true that only those who have experienced hardship know the thankfulness of rest.

Training awaited us even during the sweet, restful night. First, we had to learn how to do the laundry. We had to wash all basic clothing such as underwear by ourselves. We took our laundry to the wash place where we rubbed soap and hand-washed our own clothes. We moved onto the next training after hanging our clothes to dry. We learnt how to make our bed. The blanket had to be folded in a right angle on the bed. After we finished learning how to organize our clothes and clean the room, the instructor shouted,

"You will get some time to clean your room and personal lockers. I will inspect each room in 30 minutes. The room that scores the lowest will have to run around the sports field ten times. Begin now!"

Our squad came together under the determination that our room should be cleanest of them all. We swept, wiped, and cleaned the room with no hand resting. It was a moment of self-discovery because I hadn't even cleaned my own room back at home until this point.

Bedtime was 11:00pm. Everyone had to close their eyes, no exception. The lights turned off in all the rooms. We didn't have the energy to chat in bed because we were so tired. I fell into a deep, sweet sleep as soon as my back touched the mattress.

A day passed, then two, then three...until a week had passed. It was such an unfamiliar lifestyle and a hard time too, but it was a worthwhile and meaningful week. It felt like I would have no problem adapting to school life and I had already formed several good relationships during this short period. Even the instructors (who were quite scary at first) congratulated us for completing this training."

Create a Mental Enhancement Program

Courses at All Nations School begin with 'mental training'. Physically daunting training sessions such as close-order drill, long-distance running, trekking, mountain climbing, and martial art(taekwondo) training also carry educational importance. Although we can't go as far as to hold 'hell-week' boot camps, we can plant a challenging spirit in each of our students by giving them the experience of completing one session of mental training. This also applies to studying. Students gain the thought that studying is a challenge towards their dreams. This is what I tell our teachers:

"If there is absolutely nothing else left to do, get them to dig a hole and fill it up again. They need to experience hardship to become leaders in the future. Our children have been weakened because the environment is so soft and comfy. They get scared before getting started and they think of giving up the moment things get a little difficult. Only those with a strong mind will end up in the leading position."

Our teachers and I are constantly pondering the following: 'How can we give our children a hard time?' Since our children are living in such an overprotective environment, we need to come up with mental enhancement programs intentionally to enhance their mental power. The mental training program at our school includes:

- New student group training camp: This is a school adaptation training to fix the habits that have been made and set from the household.
- Walking trip: The entire student body and faculty walk 25~30km in May every year.
- Mountain-climbing training: This program plants confidence in the students by allowing them to experience taking on a challenge and achieving the goal.
- Half-marathon: This is the best training to enhance the mental power to break through limits.

The graduating class (12th grade) does not have a gym class. Instead, boys run 30 laps(12km) and girls run 20 laps(8km) around the school field every Saturday. The teachers run alongside them too. The following writing is a vivid account of the change of emotions and state of mind that Deborah experienced as she ran each round of the half-marathon.

"Round One. It was cold and tiresome.
Round Two. It felt doable.
Round Three. People started tossing away their jackets like snakes shedding skin.
Round Four. It was touching to see our friends encourage the ones who were lagging.
Round Five. The moon looked beautiful floating in the clear sky.
Round Six. I started wondering if I could complete the marathon. It was hard.
Round Seven. I realized that everything depended on willpower.
Round Eight. I took control of my heart and mind and started running with a joyful heart.
Round Nine. I was thankful for my healthy body that enabled me to run.
Round Ten. I had the chance to pray.
Round Eleven. I thought that boys really are boys (in terms of physical competence)
Round Twelve. I thought that we are one in heart as each individual runner began to gather and run in synch.

Round Thirteen. I was grateful for the way that we were cheering on and taking care of each other.

Round Fourteen. Second crisis, but I overcame it with will power!

Round Fifteen. I once again realized just how positive All Nations people are.

Round Sixteen. I was thankful for our teachers.

Round Seventeen. It was quite fun to run at the head of the group, and I also realized that the position came with a weird sense of responsibility.

Round Eighteen. I learnt that All Nations girls have a loud voice and an incredible lung capacity.

Round Nineteen. I felt thankful because I gained the hope that I could actually do something.

Round Twenty. I learnt the power of working together."

Many students study for the purpose of survival in the future. Thus, the pressure to do well overpowers the joy of studying. They think that they need to get good grades to go to a good university and get a good job. Studying becomes a strategy for survival. This makes way for fear to enter their hearts. Fear creates stress and obsession that smothers the students, threatens the parents, and suffocates the teachers, and it makes people resort to dishonest methods such as cheating.

Do you know what the best survival strategy is? It is to stop thinking about survival. To survive (sur+vive) is to live within a certain boundary. We need to change this. We need to surpass (sur+pass) and leap beyond the 'boundary' and into the blue ocean. I challenge the young adults who are struggling to find a job to go out of the country. I tell them to go to developing countries like Vietnam, Cambodia, and Kazakhstan rather than to fully developed countries like the United States. I advise them to take the thousands of dollars they are spending on learning English to go study in developing countries and become experts in those countries. This is the outcome of having a mindset of breaking through and 'going beyond the boundary'.

What is it that we need to pass on to our teenagers? How to live safely? The trick to getting into a top university? Those are all but survival strategies. People with weak mental power always search for the safest spots that they can find. They only want a safe life. It wouldn't be right to leave our children to tie their dreams down to that limit. We need to raise their mental power so that they may attempt new things and take on challenges.

BRAIN POWER

01

Solomon Project

One day, Michelle came to the principal's office.

"Teacher, I want to help the junior students."
"You do? Tell me more."
"It seems like some of the younger students are struggling to find the direction to study. May I open a seminar on the topic of studying?"

That was how the 'Solomon Project' began through Michelle's voluntary suggestion. The name of the project was derived from 'Proverbs of Solomon'

"As iron sharpens iron, so one person sharpens another." (Proverbs 27:17)

The Solomon Project aims to find a study method in coexistence. It aims for students to improve together. Having a competitive mindset and going solo may have its benefits in the short term, but there is a clear limit when it comes to growth. We need to look for ways to grow together. Isn't it exciting to imagine a platform of education in which students polish each other?

The Solomon Project

We hold a seminar dedicated to the topic of 'studying' about a month into each semester when the new students are just about settled. The older students are the speakers and the new students, and the teachers are the audience. As you may already know, students are influenced much more strongly by the words of their fellow students than by those of adults because they have a common understanding. Hannah is a student who asserts positive influence in various aspects including self-management, personal relations, and grades. At this seminar, Hannah came before the new students to share her thoughts on studying Chinese as a foreign language.

"What criteria do we use to assess a person's language skills in English or Chinese? We could look at their pronunciation, grades, or listening skills, but one of the most important yardsticks would be the size of their vocabulary. They will have a difficult time expressing themselves if they have a limited vocabulary, regardless of however good their pronunciation or grades may be. That is why we need to know a lot of words. Then the next question would be: how can we memorize all those words? Don't be discouraged if you are struggling to memorize everything in a short period of time. That skill varies from person to person. The important part is to retain what you've memorized for an extended period. Today, I would like to share some of my studying methods.

Firstly, there is the association method. Chinese characters are a combination of individual letters, so knowing the meaning of each letter makes it easy for us to guess the meaning of each character. This method will help you a lot when you are learning how to read.

Secondly, there's writing. Whenever a teacher gives us a repeated writing assignment, we can see that there are students who learn easily and students who need full pages of writing before they can grasp the concept. This is a difference in concentration. A student who only wants to finish the assignment as soon as possible would wander in their mind while doing the assignment and thus will take longer to memorize the words. Therefore, it is important to focus on what you are writing and to be conscious of the fact that you are memorizing the material as you are writing it.

Thirdly, there is the self-testing method. You get tensed up when you take the writing quizzes, right? However, there is no reason to tense up when you are giving yourself a mock exam. Testing yourself, realizing your weaknesses, and relearning what you got wrong will help reduce the number of errors you make on an actual test and thus stabilize your performance.

Fourthly, there's frequent practice. For this method, I encourage you to talk with our native teachers. Native speakers have the best understanding of the application of each word, and our teachers are all so kind and eagerly waiting for us to come talk to them. They will teach us ten things for every question we bring them, so you will soon see a clear difference in knowledge. Finally, there is repeated practice. This method requires you to constantly remind yourself of what you've learnt or to carry around a vocabulary card stack so that you can reteach yourself several times. Although it is difficult to mentally recall all the things that you've learnt or to carry your notes everywhere, the return for this method is quite high compared to the trouble since you retain a lot more.

While there are many more memorization methods and a different method suitable for each person, I hope that this introduction will help you to find the best way for you to memorize."

It feels like our students have surpassed their teachers. Who wouldn't perk their ears when someone is talking so coherently based on their experience? The Solomon Project is more than a one-time seminar. The seminar acts to create a studying atmosphere among the students and to make way for steps to follow. Students who are struggling in certain subjects are paired with study mates, and lowerclassmen are paired into mentor-mentee groups with upperclassmen.

Making a Study Mate

We pair together 'study mates' once the seminars are over. This is a commonly used method among the Jewish people. You may have heard about the 'yeshiva' which is basically a Jewish library. The first thing that Jewish people do when they enter a yeshiva is to find a study partner. The partner does not necessarily have to be a friend. Once they find a partner, they study together and engage in heated debates as they exchange questions and answers. Imagine hundreds of people debating in pairs. The library is as noisy as a Sunday market. This debate-study method is advantageous because arguments are naturally organized and memorized through the string of questions and answers. Furthermore, it expands each person's spectrum of thought since they get to hear the opinions of another person.

Most students in East Asia tend to prefer to study by listening and memorizing without questioning. Platforms for debate need to be made for them. However, once a general structure is provided, they do it and do it well even if they are only doing it because 'they have to'. That is why we decided to implement the 'study mate' method. The following 'study mate' experience is an extract from the story shared by Young-Jin during the Solomon Project.

"...so, what I want to tell you is how precious your study mate is. I wouldn't be who I am today without my study mates. We helped each other in times of need and did not hesitate to give sharp words of advice. Thankfully, my friends did not get hurt by my words of advice and simply accepted them although they could have been received unpleasantly. We should appreciate the advice of our friends and accept it as words of love. Also, if you want true friends, offer words of advice."

The strength of having a study mate lies in the fact that it is a relationship of support and not competition. We need to learn from our partner's pool of knowledge and share what we know with as many people as possible. We need to help each other out because we are the people who are going to change the world as well as the ones to support other such people. There are teachers and 'study mates' at our school to whom we can turn to for help. Do not miss out on all the things that you can gain from this wonderful environment.

Double the Brain Power
Through the Mentoring System

Michelle is the student who first suggested the 'Solomon Project' when she was in 11th grade. She also suggested the 'mentoring system' as we proceeded with the Solomon Project. This is how our school came to have this beautiful tradition. There are times when teachers come up with policies to lead the children, but there are also many times when students come up with a good suggestion that eventually becomes part of the school system in the process. The entire student body becomes much more creative and happier when you recognize and encourage their potential.

Our mentoring system proceeds as follows: Michelle is in charge of overall mentoring, and two head mentors and 20~30 mentors divide into teams whereby each team takes responsibility of a lower grade class. Mentee underclassmen exchange notes with their mentors in order to keep the conversation going. We adopted this method of conversation because, aside from scheduling regular meetings, this method is far more effective than trying to arrange a meeting time at each occasion. Head mentors also exchange notes with the mentors to discuss any situation or difficulties they're facing and to share any effective ideas. While this may seem to form a pyramidal structure at first glance, it is actually a radial structure. It is very efficient and organized, and I'm just proud to see such a structured mentoring system operated by the wisdom and discussions of the students. Let's hear about the beginning and the effects of the mentoring system from Michelle.

"There is a four-character idiom that every single student at our school knows about. 啐啄同時! This means that a chick and a hen peck at the shell simultaneously from both the inside and out when the chick is about to hatch. Just like how a chick requires the mother hen's help to be born into the world, we also need someone to help us outside our shells along with our own persistence and hard work to mature into leaders who make a good influence on this world.

I believe that mentoring is the 啐啄同時 between our friends who have already broken out of their shell and those who are about to. The mother hen does not peck unwillingly or half-heartedly. She does it with anticipation for the chicks that will crack out of their shells. This is the same for our mentor friends. Our mentors voluntarily dedicate themselves to helping the lowerclassmen although nobody had forced them to take on that duty. This warmth isn't limited to just our mentors. The 'mentoring system' of our school is the embodiment of love itself.

I think so, not because this is my school, but because I see the beautiful hearts that are eager to share what they have, and the hard work put in by each student in hopes to grow together. That is why I am thankful for today and hopeful for tomorrow."

Mentoring is more than the simple exchange of questions and answers regarding study material. Students share their studying methods, explain the characteristics of each step of a studying process, and provide counseling on how to make further improvements. In other words, students donate their wisdom to the younger students. Through the mentoring system, students learn the secret of the win/win synergy where you and I both get to win.

When studying, we need to find a way to make our brain dance. We need to figure out how to 'Study Smart' instead of 'Study Hard'. Working hard isn't necessarily equivalent to giving it your all. We need to find the way where we all- and not just I- get to win. As such, the purpose of the Solomon Project lies in this sharing of wisdom. Wisdom surges like a spring when it is shared. We need to raise our children into springs of wisdom.

02

Utilize
Brain Science

The brain science of study skills has also seen astounding developments. Gone are the days when we just sat down and studied hard. Parents are under the delusion that the time that students spend awake in front of their desks equals study time. This delusion tires the brain and sometimes causes the student to be angry or bored. It is necessary to adjust the definition of 'studying' from the perspective of brain science.

"Studying is the process in which a neural network is created in the brain through an external stimulus."

The brain is the most active organ in our body which is responsible for 20% of total oxygen consumption despite weighing only around

1.4 kg. What decides the function of the brain? We need to have the following basic knowledge about brain cells to better understand the mechanism of brain science. Although we may be unfamiliar with the vocabulary below, we should memorize it as general knowledge.

Terms & Roles Related to Cranial Nerves	
Term	Role
Neuron	the cell responsible for the exchange of information
Glial Cell	enhances the role of the neuron
Synapse	the connecting gap between neurons
Neurotransmitter	transmits signals at the synapse
Brain-Derived Neurotrophic Factor (BDNF)	involved in neuron survival and growth

Neurotransmitters & Roles		
Neurotransmitter	Role	Symptom
Dopamine	stimulates pleasure	high enthusiasm
Noradrenaline	stimulates shock, anger, etc. in the central nervous system	anxiety
Serotonin	stimulates emotions	healthy mood
Acetylcholine	helps activate the nerve cell	clearness of mind
L-Glutamine	plays the traditional role of transferring information	same as normal
GABA	suppresses excitation	relaxation
Endorphin	emotional numbing	comfort

Our brain cells comprise of approximately 10% of neurons and 90% of glial cells. Its structure is as shown in the following diagram, and it exchanges information through the numerous protrusions that extend from the cell body. The part that receives information from other neurons is called a 'dendrite' and the part that sends information is called an 'axon'. The wrapping around the axon is the 'myelin' from glial cells.

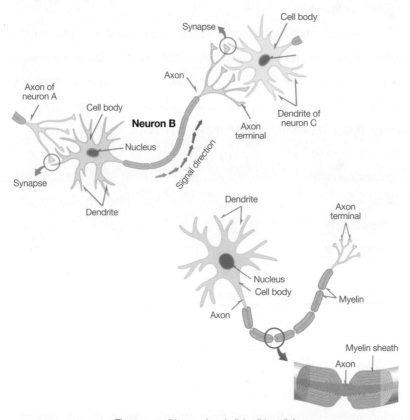

The nerve cell 'neuron' and glial cell 'myelin'

Functions of the glial cell include surrounding the neuron and providing physical support, supplying oxygen and nutrients to the neuron, insulating the neuron and preventing leakage of information, repairing damaged parts, and removing dead neurons. In other words, neurons cannot function properly without glial cells. We need to practice repeatedly when learning a new sport, memorizing vocabulary of a foreign language, or solving math problems because repetition builds myelin.

In order to make our brains smarter, we need to optimize the combination of healthy neurons, glial cells, neurotransmitters, synapses, and BDNF. Ultimately, we need to have good control over our brains to maximize the effects of studying. The methodology can be summarized into the following key words:

- continuously
- freshly
- repeatedly
- peacefully

The Mechanism of Learning

Neurons are the principal nerve cells that comprise brain cells. Humans are born with approximately 100 billion neurons. The splendid information transmission function of neurons allows us to move our bodies and think. Neurons are made of a cell body, dendrites that receive information, and axons that send information.

The cell body manages the cell, combines signals to create a new signal that is sent to the axon, and creates and supplies energy so that the neuron may continue to work well. The dendrite receives signals from other neurons and sends them to the cell body. Information received through the dendrite passes through the cell body and reach the axon. The axon connects with the dendrite of the next neuron and transfers the signal via the synapse. The synapse refers to the connective gap between the axon terminal and the dendrites of the next neuron. There is no physical connection, and the gap is about one millionth of an inch. Neurotransmitters in this gap transfer information by converting electrical signals into chemical signals. The information is passed on by repeatedly changing forms as electrical signals in the neuron and chemical signals in the synapse. As such, information is transferred from neuron A to neuron B, then from neuron B to neuron C to create a neural network.

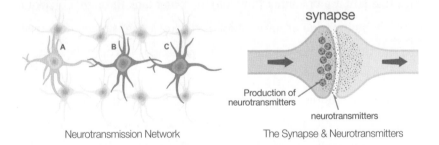

synapse

Production of neurotransmitters

neurotransmitters

Neurotransmission Network   The Synapse & Neurotransmitters

Neurotransmitters that are deeply connected with studying include adrenaline(excitement), noradrenaline(anger), dopamine (pleasure, satisfaction), and serotonin(happiness). The neurotransmitter that influences studying the most is serotonin. On the other hand, if we take too much stress, it will hinder our brain activity. It also prevents balanced production of neurotransmitters. Therefore, it is necessary to control cortisol, a stress hormone, to improve study efficiency and creativity.

Happiness is Key

The brain can be intimidated when exposed to stress. People who live in high-stress environments tend to be constantly low in spirit. Results are not as satisfying compared to the number of hours invested and anger starts to build up. They get the urge to break anything within their reach. Why does this happen? It's because a disrupter appeared in their brain. It's the overproduction of cortisol or noradrenaline showing on the outside. In other words, the neural circuit in the brain has stiffened which in turn disrupted the smooth flow of information. Just like how water cannot flow into the water tank through a blocked pipe, the knowledge or information is having a hard time getting past the short-term memory point in the hippocampus to get to the storage unit in the frontal lobe.

There is a solution, though. The problem can be solved by normalizing the connection and flow between the nerve cells by removing the cause of stress and replacing the disruptors with good neurotransmitters. In other words, we need to increase serotonin to drill through the neural circuit. It's no surprise that the effect of studying is low compared to the hours of investment when you are trying to pass knowledge through a blocked road. The author of 'Serotonin Hara'(meaning 'Dominate Serotonin') Doctor Si-Hyeong Lee explains in detail three important characteristics of serotonin in his book as follows. Firstly, serotonin is called the regulating material because it gives liveliness and energy by interfering with sentimental or emotional actions, sleep, memory, and appetite control. Secondly, it is also called the studying material because it regulates the overproduction of angry or extreme neurotransmitters such as adrenaline and dopamine, whereby having a calming effect and increasing creativity and concentration. Furthermore, serotonin is called the happiness material because it allows you to feel a calm happiness as opposed to explosive joy by dopamine. Let's list the ways that serotonin affects our lives:

- It calms the mind.
- It allows us to find peacefulness from a state of stress, excitement, or anger.
- It makes depressing emotions disappear.
- It makes us lively through loving and happy emotions.
- It increases our self-esteem as well as resilience to difficulties.
- Pessimistic emotions are replaced with optimistic emotions.
- It has a positive influence on personal relationships.
- It improves concentration thereby increasing the effect of studying.

Therefore, it is necessary to create a serotonin-rich environment for our children or students no matter what. So, what do we need to do to create a serotonin-rich environment? I present to you the method that we use at the All Nations School.

Can you recall the keywords to control your brain? Creating a serotonin environment can be connected to the keyword 'peacefully'. Remember this keyword if you want your child or student to study well. The efficiency of studying can be maximized when the spirit and heart are at peace.

Happiness Flows with the Music

At our school, we place particular importance on our music lessons. That's why we have a significantly larger number of music teachers. We have teachers who have majored in piano, voice, string instruments, and conducting, as well as other teachers who excel in applied music such as electric or bass guitar who play a significant role. Students who are skilled in any instrument are also given the opportunity to instruct other students.

Our school sees value in music because having music nearby always makes for a happy school life. That's why we have plenty of lively orchestra, choir, and band activities. Music is part of our students' daily lives. Even the teachers enjoy practicing for choir during lunch breaks.

One day, we received a call from Hope City Office of Education. They asked if we would like to attend the art festival as a choir. We participated casually since we practiced quite regularly- but lo and

Performances at the National Choir Competition

behold, we received first prize. That was when the pressure started to creep up. We had to represent Hope City at the Provincial Competition. We received first prize at that competition also and wound up preparing for the nationwide competition. We prepared two songs, 'Lion King' and 'Joyful Joyful', and headed to the competition venue. This particular art festival, which took place every three years under the organization of the Ministry of Education, was a competition of the highest level and was also known as the arts Olympiad for middle and high school students. At this huge, week-long competition where over 7,000 students came from all over the country to represent 31 cities, we experienced the miracle of receiving the grand prize. This prize was invaluable to us because the entire student body had come together to prepare for this event: participating students had practiced in unison and students who couldn't take part had supported by praying and preparing props.

Weekly Tests and a Livelihood Graph

We have weekly tests during the first year after entering the school. This is an assessment of what each student has learnt in the past week. Students are encouraged to take it as a challenge against themselves without worrying about their class rank. This policy has many benefits. Most schools grade their students through a midterm and final exam which often causes students to fall into the pit of last-minute preparation. This doesn't do much help towards long term memory because stress causes the overproduction of cortisol which eventually damages the hippocampal, the part of the brain that is responsible for short term memory. That is why students forget everything they've learnt once they leave the exam room.

However, weekly tests are different. Students experience challenges, tension, and accomplishment each week. Weekly tests pressure the brain and enable active studying. Students are not coerced to study against their will but are led to practice studying proactively. Wouldn't it be more stressful to have exams every week? Not at all. While students can get stressed out by midterms or finals because they are ranked based on their comparative scores, weekly tests are tests in which each student's scores are compared only to their own. For example, students are motivated to increase their score by 5 points or to change their study habits. Whereas comparing to others leads to a state of constant tiredness, comparing to oneself leads to improvement from yesterday.

There is another benefit to the weekly tests. It allows us to check the emotional changes that each student undergoes. The weekly test graph is not a simple recording of grades. For instance, if a student who had achieved high grades in the first week receives progressively lower grades after some time, we might look into issues such as homesickness, friendships, illness, or worries. Since the weekly tests are taken every week, it can provide quite a detailed insight into a student's emotional fluctuation, any family conflicts, or state of health. Therefore, we can say that the 'grade graph' is also a 'livelihood graph'.

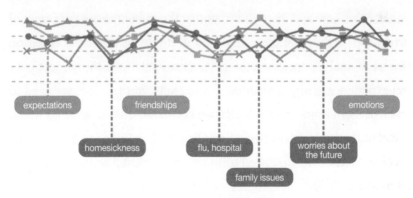

Grades plot the student's livelihood graph

Each student's grade graph is unique just as how each person's fingerprint is different. Let's look at the following graph.

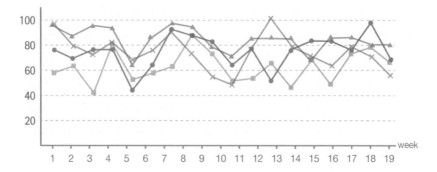

You can observe high fluctuations week by week. The graph spikes up and down like an irregular saw blade. What can we say about this student's grades? Can we simply calculate the average score and say that this student's grade is 60%? The fact that they are able to achieve high scores here and there shows us that the students have the potential to do well if they put their heart into it. It tells us that there is reason for us to analyze the cause of the fluctuations. First, the student may be experiencing high emotional fluctuations. In that case, we need to consult them immediately. When we consulted this student, we found out that the student was having conflicts with their friend and parents. In such a case, we first need to touch the students' heart so that they may restore peace.

Here's another example. This student's grades were on a constant low for the first two months. However, everyone got a big shock when the student's grades shot up in week 10 and continued to stay high. We investigated the 'before' and 'after' shots of the student's life and were even more surprised to learn that the student used to be an ill-tempered and bad-mouthed student. Their personality and grades had improved drastically at the same time. They no longer used profane words and were eager to learn from their friends. The teachers discovered that the cause of this positive transformation was an 'exemplary roommate'. As they lived together, the student had naturally observed the lifestyle of their high scoring, exemplary roommate, and had begun the 'follow-whatever-he-does project'. They acquired a good study method which led to a parade of high scores.

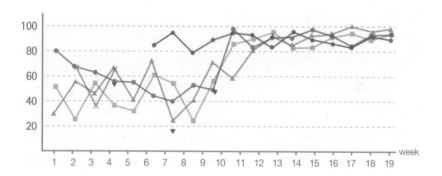

Have you heard about the concept of 'dopamine enhanced learning'? Experiencing a sense of accomplishment leads to the secretion of dopamine which in turn triggers emotions of joy and pleasure. This is followed by the desire to experience such pleasures once more. This is called dopamine enhanced learning, where a student who has accomplished a learning goal continues to study on their own even without being nagged due to the vitalization of the brain. In this case we say that the enhanced learning cycle has begun.

Let's look at a third example. This student is stable and receives good grades. Their graph doesn't vary that much. We can see that this student is very stable in mind. However, we can suspect that there might be a problem if the graph is excessively high and stable.

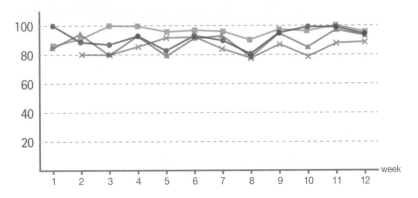

This student showed a self-centered tendency in their desire to win against others. How do we approach such a student? We need to help them inspect their purpose of studying. We need to widen their heart so that they may help others instead of studying to win against them. From this point onwards, all the teachers begin to help the student. They work closely with the parents to combine the life history, family background, and history of the child's education within the family to enter the 'transformation' process. This continues alongside gratitude training, consultations to solve visible problems, and consultations regarding purpose orientation. The student is helped to become a leader.

This student was changed thanks to the hard work of the teachers. Their friendship improves as well as their grades. They became warm-hearted students who shared their talents with the younger students. This student was Michelle, the student who suggested the Solomon Project and the mentoring system. I remember the prickly impression she gave off when she first joined our school. Now she looks brighter than ever.

It was during a seminar for Solomon Project when Michelle tossed the following question at the new students,

"Why do you study?"

Many new students gave obvious answers. To succeed, to achieve their dream, to get a job, to win in the competition…. After hearing the answers, Michelle gave her opinion.

"I think that studying is something I do to expand my influence."

Expanding your field of study is equivalent to expanding your influence. Wouldn't a person who speaks both English and Chinese assert more influence than a person who has studied only English? Studying with this mindset would undoubtedly lead to higher learning efficiency. We are so proud of Michelle for realizing this at such a young age.

Stimulate the Brain through
Discussion-based Classes.

We cannot be satisfied here after coming this far. There is nothing better to stimulate the brain and to trigger thoughts than debates(discussions). The brain is super stimulated when we think of supporting evidence for our argument and building logic to rebut the opponent's argument. That is why we came up with discussion-based classes. However, there was one problem: Koreans find discussions to be awkward. They participate in debate quite timidly, worrying, 'What if my argument is wrong?' or 'What would my friends think of me if I said this?'. However, we couldn't scold the reserved students since that would cause them to be intimidated even further. Was there a way to make the students participate actively? After various attempts, we changed the class formation from having one lecture per lesson time to having a collective of classes in small groups of five to six students. This way, students felt freer to speak up since they didn't have to address a roomful of classmates.

Of course, this method alone wasn't enough. We had to change the lesson plan drastically. The teacher's lecture was reduced from 40 minutes to 20 minutes and the remaining time was given to the students. Students would gather in their groups, discuss, and solve the problem that the teacher had given them beforehand, and present the outcome with the rest of the class. Then students from other groups would ask questions or give their opinions. Teachers would give comments or guidelines as necessary.

This process brings students to participate in class extensively and the effect of learning is multiplied tenfold. No one can slack off since everybody has a set role. Students rarely fall asleep. Academic achievement increases since students can receive immediate assistance from their teammates whenever they have an inquiry. Class concentration increases and in-class memorization increases. Instead, teachers need to prepare much more than they used to for rote learning classes. Class quality does a complete 180. Students become more interested in active learning than in passive spoon-feeding and can experience the joy of learning.

Last semester, our school opened our discussion-based classes for all the parents to observe. Numerous parents came to sit in. Yana Wang, the teacher in charge of 7th grade Chinese language education, skillfully distributed the pre-study topics that she had prepared for each small group, explained the core task, and guided the students to discuss among themselves. After a set amount of time, some students came up to the board to write the summary of the discussion topic and some students asked questions on the presentations. There were moments of high-tensioned debate when students stood by their opinions and rebuttals. Then there was a group that quickly-wittedly presented their topic in the form of a short skit, making the class burst into laughter as if the tension from before never existed. The amazing fact is that all of this is done by the students themselves. Then what do the teachers do? The teacher gives comments or corrects anything that is incorrectly expressed during each group's presentation. The teacher also guides the class in making the final comprehensive summary of the contents of the lesson. Thus, the students are the owners of the lesson, and the teachers are their coach.

Let's look into an example. Xianming was a very introverted and quiet student. However, his presentation skills improved immensely after starting discussion-based classes. His nickname these days is 'debate master'. The following is Xianming's experience in the discussion-based classes.

There are many distinct features in the education of our school. However, the most recent feature is the discussion-based lesson. The students were very happy when we first heard that we were to begin 'discussion-based classes' because of one reason: we would get more time to talk with our friends. I was also very excited. We were assigned to our groups, and I was very pleased with my group members and my seat.

Classes became the only time when we got to chat and have fun with our friends while sharing our opinions and thoughts. From that day onward, the teachers distributed the discussion topic the day before for pre-study so that the discussion-based class could proceed more efficiently. Initially, I wasn't happy when we got our first discussion topics because I was used to rote learning and was yet to experience the fun of studying. Despite it all, the principal put a lot of emphasis on having discussions and he slowly made improvements to the lesson through the strong determination of the teachers slowly making improvements. As the year passed by, I became more accustomed and more active.

I truly enjoyed sharing my opinions with my friends, debating on the same topic, and viewing a problem from various perspectives. It was helpful to receive the discussion topic beforehand for prestudy. The textbook became easier to read and easier to memorize.

The current discussion-based classes helped me to study more efficiently and to tackle problems from a different perspective. I am grateful for this education."

Although we went through some trial and error, we were able to secure the discussion-based classes through the hard work of our faculty and the participation of our students. It is needless to say that our students' grades have improved since this new style of education was introduced. Furthermore, we saw a huge improvement in the concentration levels of students who had previously struggled to stay focused.

Albert Einstein is a genius that everyone on earth recognizes. His words are still cited by many. I would like to quote the following two sentences as well.

"The important thing is to not stop questioning. Curiosity has its

own reason for existing."
"Imagination is more important than knowledge. Knowledge is limited. Imagination encircles the world."

That's right. The brain thinks. Therefore, it exists. We need to make the students think to activate their brains. Thoughts act as constant stimuli for the brain. Can you recall? The brain science keywords that increase the efficiency of studying are 'happiness' and 'stimulation'. Before we nag our children or students to study, we need to try to scratch the itch in the brain, allow them to experience plenty of happiness, and stimulate the brain to make the nerve circuits of the brain sturdier.

03

Ways to Smarten
the Brain

"Hello. My name is Daniel, and I am a Jew. All the Daniels on the surface of the earth (including Daniel Radcliffe) are named after me. I was born 2600 years ago. My motherland Judah was conquered by Babylon. At that time, I was a teenager full of dreams. I was taken captive from Jerusalem and brought to Babylon where I began life as a slave. That was when the royal academy was established. It was a special three-year course. Its goal was probably to select children of royal or noble descent from the conquered countries and to educate them to become puppet leaders. My three Jewish friends and I were selected to live at the school and study. The dormitory was great, and we were able to receive top treatment. It was a multicultural school, including nobles from Egypt. We decided to study hard with the anticipation that our country will one day regain independence. I tried hard to keep the faith that I had inherited from my homeland since birth. I took time to pray silently towards Jerusalem three times a day. This enabled me to manage my time and myself thoroughly. I was able to study quite well at the royal academy since I had the traditional Jewish lifestyle habits. Of course, we weren't without problems. The biggest problem was eating. We had to eat meat and drink wine every day. So, my friends and I made a request to the manager. We asked him to keep us on a diet of vegetables, beans, and water. The manager hesitated and told us that he was worried that the king might get mad at him. So, we told him to experiment with it for ten days. Ten days later, we compared the complexion between us and four other students who were on a diet of meat and wine. He saw that our complexion was much brighter and livelier. Meat versus vegetables. Alcohol versus water. Isn't it clear which is better? - Vegetables and water, of course. Our skin was literally glimmering. Plenty of hydration played a big part in keeping our bodies healthy.

Our grades? Awesome, of course. The four of us took 1st place to 4th. The other students who drank alcohol and ate meat daily and didn't get enough exercise could not compare to us. We spoke several languages and were abundant in our wisdom. We learnt in the strongest country in the world and became some of the greatest wise men of the era. All this was due to the lifestyle habits that we inherited from our fathers and grandfathers. None of this was due to our own merits. We can only thank the Lord our God whom our ancestors have worshiped throughout the years."

(This is the reconstituted story of the biblical character, Dainel, in storytelling format.)

The entire world is focusing on the education methods of the Jewish people. Jewish education takes place in discussion format between parents and children with Torah or Talmud as the medium before they go to sleep every night. This debate that naturally takes place in the home provides motivation to study and stimulates the brain whereby enhancing memorization skills and creativity. In other words, brain power can be enhanced when we activate the neural network in the brain through questions and debates.

That's not all. The secret to brain power can also be found in their lifestyle habits. Habits including food culture, the normalization of self-discipline, and praying habits can increase their brain power. In other words, their lives are surrounded by an environment that enhances brain power. Among it all, one thing that we must focus on is their eating habits.

Let's inspect the eating habits of our family. Don't we skip breakfast regularly and mainly rely on a diet of meat and instant foods? Most dads in Korea are pressured by their workplace (by their colleagues to be exact) to drink his weight and return home late and drunk. Moms are immersed in TV dramas. When the child returns home, the parents give them some fruit or juice and nag them to study. The situation can only be explained with the expression: "Oh my God." Children in Korea are incredible because they can break their backs studying even in such an environment.

Jewish people train their children to maintain a strict eating habit. Food that they can eat is separated from food that they cannot, and they use ingredients that are clean and fresh. Brain power begins from such eating habits. It is incredibly important to improve our eating habits if we want to enhance our brain power. There is a reason why we emphasize the importance of living in dorms. It is because teachers can correct the eating habits of children at school if their parents are unable to do so due to various reasons. We cannot talk about brain power without mentioning the nutrient and oxygen supply to the brain. Additionally, it is as important to rest the brain. The brains of the students in East Asia are horribly worn out. They need to be picked up again. They need to gain untiring brain power. This will be covered more in the later chapters of 'power six.'

Daniel maintained a diet based on vegetables. It isn't that Jews don't eat meat. However, Daniel decided to consume only vegetables and a lot of water given the circumstances (where eating the king's food was like idol worship). This story hides a big brain power secret. There is a Jewish national food called the 'falafel'. It is a vegetable ball made mainly with bean powder, parsley, garlic, and onions. There is also a sauce that the Jewish people commonly enjoy called 'hummus'. Hummus is a sauce made of mashed chickpeas, garlic, olive oil, and salt and it fantastically elevates all dishes. Go ahead and try some falafel, olives, or salad with some pita bread. It is a brain power-enhancing menu that is delicious and rich in vegetable protein. It is like the traditional Korean dish 'bibimbap'. To think about it, Korean traditional eating habits were brain power friendly. However, as society underwent modernization and urbanization, traditional eating habits were replaced with eating habits focused on instant foods and fat-filled meat products.

The brain can be seen as a vegetarian. Bo-Geun Jang, a PD and professor, interviewed Cyberkinetics and the Harvard University Center for Brain Science Neuroimaging to produce the documentary, 'Another Universe, Brain'. His book 'Parents Who Save the Brain, Parents Who Kill the Brain' depicts just how much the brain is affected by a vegetarian diet. According to the book, a research team in Boston, United States measured the IQs of vegetarian children and found a whopping average of 116. Children of similar age who weren't on a vegetarian diet showed to be lagging in intellectual development by approximately one year. In another experiment on mice, mice that were injected with a plant-based fatty acid called linolenic acid displayed higher memory and patience than mice that were injected with animal-based fatty acids.

The brain requires unsaturated fatty acids to become smarter. This is more abundant in plants than in animals. While unsaturated fatty acids make nerve cells more flexible whereby improving brain function, the saturated fatty acids and cholesterol included in meat decreases the secretion of neurotransmitters such as serotonin that allows the smooth connection between nerve cells within the brain whereby decreasing the learning ability of the brain. Furthermore, it narrows blood vessels in the brain, causing problems related to blood flow and oxygen supply, causing the aging of the brain.

We decided to apply the eating habits of the Jews. Food that is clean according to Jewish rules is called 'Kosher', which means 'food that is fit to consume'. This is listed in the book of Leviticus in the Torah. You can find several interesting facts when you read this book. For instance, animal intestines and oils(fats) cannot be consumed. These should be burnt at the altar when making an offering to God.

Many people in Korea eat fat-filled pork belly and giblets. They like wagyu, which is marbled rather than steak with little fat. The more marbled meat, the better the grade is recognized as meat in these countries. However, it has been scientifically proven since then that it is better for your health to stay away from these meat cuts. All animals maintain a body temperature between 38~42 degrees Celsius which is 2~4 degrees higher than the average human body temperature. When animal fats are absorbed by the human body, the animal fats become stickier in the comparatively colder environment and causes blood clots and cardiovascular diseases.

Kosher products are receiving significant international popularity these days. Sometimes, products that receive Kosher certification are seen as cleanly produced organic products. Kosher requires cattle to also be raised on clean feed. At a time when environmental hormones in cattle is a severe issue, Jewish eating habits are viewed as more than a culture and are recognized to have global product value.

The Daniel Project

Our school has dedicated one month each semester as a healthy diet month with food items such as brown rice and tofu. While we make sure to include vegetables and fruits in our regular meals, this month is a time during which we stay clear of processed foods and stick to a vegetable-centered diet. No student is left behind since students eat all three meals at the school cafeteria. Won't students get stressed out because of this project since they cannot have any spicy or fried food, snacks, or ice cream? Not at all. In fact, many students experience the beneficial effects of this project.

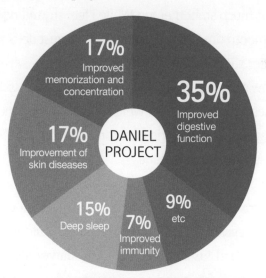

The result of Daniel Project

One of our students, Yeju, visited me about two weeks after we started the Daniel Project.

"Teacher, it has been two weeks since the Daniel Project and I can already feel the difference in my body."

"Really? Tell me about it."

"First, I doze off less during class. I think my concentration is improving. Also, I used to have a hard time falling asleep during nighttime. Now I fall asleep as soon as I lie down on my bed. I really think my concentration will increase tremendously if this keeps up for the next two months."

"It surely will. Many other students have experienced increased concentration levels and higher grades."

"My skin is much smoother too. While I feel shy telling you this, I have a "smooth time" in the toilet too. All I must do is sit, and it's like a water slide. Teehee!"

"You know why it's easier for you to go to the toilet, right? Vegetables have a lot of fiber which helps in bowel movements. That's why it helps to get rid of chronic constipation."

"I'm so happy these days, hehe."

We are surrounded by food products that deteriorate our brain power. The biggest problem is the abundance and easy access of processed food and instant food. All the additives also create many problems. The trans fats in these food products are also a big nuisance.

It weakens the cell wall, creates infections, and intervenes in the composition of neurotransmitters. Studying is the process of enhancing the connectivity between the synapses of healthy brain nerve cells, so imagine the impact of deteriorated serotonin production. It would lead to deteriorated brain function. Go ahead and enjoy instant food if you want to mess up your brain.

The Daniel Project takes place for a month each semester. Students who struggle at first participate eagerly after experiencing the effect.

To raise awareness of the importance of healthy food, we hold a cooking contest every year to introduce healthy food from around the world.

Stay Clear from the Trap of Addiction

Let's return to the story of Daniel. All the students aside from Daniel and his friends enjoyed the abundant supply of meat and wine. (While there is a big difference between their culture and our modern cultures) Imagine a classroom full of drunk students. Would it even be possible to study in such an environment? Something we need to focus on is that alcohol, unlike water, is addictive. Addiction results in the damage of brain cells. It doesn't matter whether the subject of addiction is alcohol, cigarettes, internet, or smartphones- they all come down to the same result. BBC broadcasted the research results of the Chinese Academy of Science that the brain damage of alcoholics is like the brain damage of internet addicts. Doctor Rei Hao from Chinese Academy of Science did a special brain scan on a variety of addicts and discovered that internet addicts show damage in the white matter of the brain like the damage shown in those with drug addictions, porn addictions, or impulse control disorders. This means that the part of the white matter that is related to the production and handling of emotions, executive functioning, decision making, and cognitive control.

Team Kim Sang-Eun of Bundang Seoul National University Hospital, Korea, has also published research results that over users of internet games show brain activity that is similar to the brain activity of drug addicts. This means that excessive gaming can develop from a behavioral addiction into a disease in the cranial nerve.

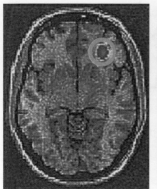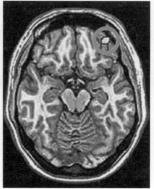

Brain of cocaine addicted(left) and brain of internet game addicted(right). Both sides exhibit the same neuronal mechanism in relation to self-control ability. Provided by Bundang Seoul National University Hospital

Then, what are the things that cause damage to our student's brain? Internet games, of course. Internet games have a critical impact on the brain whether it is played on a PC or smartphone. Professor Mori Akino from Nihon University, Japan, measured the brainwave activity of 240 people between the ages 6~29 when they played computer games. The results showed a huge decrease in the activity at the frontal lobe, the part of the brain that acts as the supreme commander. Delayed development of the frontal lobe will cause an adverse effect in the development of the entire brain. Furthermore, playing a lot of computer games causes an excess secretion of dopamine, a pleasure material, increasing the risk of addiction. Hypersecretion of dopamine makes the person crave even greater pleasure and causes the person to find everyday life uninteresting. Finally, addiction causes the person to neglect their studies and personal relations. Just like a car with a broken brake running downhill, the person ends up damaging their brain.

Implementing the Brain-Love Program

People who have trouble controlling their use of addictive appliances (computers, smartphones, gaming devices, etc.) would be better off getting rid of them. However, the surrounding environment doesn't quite help. We are constantly attached to our smartphones and our streets are lined with PC rooms.... so, we decided to start by changing the environment. Our school has applied a Clean Zone policy. Our students do not go to PC rooms, do not play online games, do not carry around smartphones (as we mentioned before), and limit the use of MP3s or MP4s. Drinking and smoking is prohibited of course. This is the 'Brain-Love Program' that we have been abiding by since our school opened.

The Brain-Love Program where we do not use addictive appliances. This policy has been in place since the opening of our school.

Minho is the graduate of our school currently attending 'School of Visual Arts' in Manhattan, one of the top universities in the design field. He was a student who was addicted to Internet games in the past. He shared the following story of his one year of electronics-free experience.

"Looking back at my life in another school before my coming to All Nations School, I spent seven periods a day studying at school and practiced art after school. I went to PC rooms or karaoke with my friends if I had any remaining free time and went home late at night every day. Thinking back, it feels like I was a bad son. I was a narrow-minded person who cannot see the larger world like a frog in the well. So, when I left my comfort zone to come to the All Nations School and made many new friends, I gained a lot of interest in studying and became passionate about becoming a good leader.

I used to think that the fact that I had attended an arts school was something to be proud about and was full of myself for quite a while even after I moved to this school. However, this pridefulness shrunk as I saw the fellow students here. There are so many well-rounded, talented students. I came to realize just how narrow and shallow my perspective was as I continued to live at this school. So, I decided to forget everything that I had learnt from the arts high school and start anew.

I used to love playing computer games. Games are made to be irresistible, complete with immediate rewards. I loved the pleasures that it offered even though I was aware of it. However, now I know. The future will remain unsure if I continue to pursue such pleasures."

In this country, the law prohibits children under the age of 18 from entering PC game rooms. I think this is a very appropriate measure seeing how more and more students are becoming addicted to gaming. If there is a student who is having a hard time focusing on their studies because of their lifestyle habits, we need to provide them with protection and proper guidance. Instead of just telling students who lack delayed gratification to stop playing games, we need to provide them with the right environment.

Power Four

MORAL POWER

01

The Competitive Edge of Honesty

According to media reports, famous cram schools in Asian countries are said to have leaked SAT questions (university entrance exam for U.S. universities) almost every year. How bad does it have to get for word to go around that the criteria to become a popular instructor is based on their ability to sneak out questions? The situation has worsened so much that American universities do not trust the SAT scores presented by Korean and Chinese students. It is as if people whose life goal is to get the top score and to be admitted to a top university don't feel guilt for their illegal actions anymore. Of course, this problem is not exclusive to Asians. We often see people from all parts of the world report to dishonest actions in order to win the competition, because of their ethical insensitivity, or even just for the thrill.

Let's talk about the Unites States? The FBI announced the results of an investigation into the College Admissions Scandal in 2019. Rich parents including Hollywood stars paid huge amounts to the admission fraudster who assured admission to the prestigious universities. The fraud methods were very diverse. Taking surrogate tests, doing SAT score manipulation, giving bribes, manipulating a career, etc. In a nutshell, America's morality fell to the ground.

Many psychologists have continued to do research to get a psychological answer as to why people cheat. One interesting result showed that people who have lower self-control have a higher possibility of resorting to cheating. This experiment was conducted in 2002 on 107 college students.

What about teenagers? In 2004, Finn and Frone presented the results of their research on the learning ability and self-esteem of students who cheat, conducted on 316 teenagers. (see J. Education Research, 97, No 3, 115-122, 2004) 'Cheating' as defined in this study included sneaking a peak at someone else's test paper, copying homework, asking someone else to do their homework, and plagiarism. Only 12% of the students did not cheat, and 11% of the 88% that had cheated turned out to be high-frequency cheaters. This research revealed that the higher the frequency of cheating, the lower the self-efficiency and learning ability.

To draw the conclusion on this cheating phenomenon, people whose aim is accomplishment cannot decline the benefit that is before their eyes. However, people who want to become the master of their field put importance in the process. Since these people value the process, they become successful in the end even if they may take a little more time. Thus, to cheat or not to cheat is a difference that comes from the strength of our moral muscle.

As briefly touched upon in the preceding chapter, our school has already experienced the competitive edge of the moral muscle first hand when we faced temptation and conflict in the process of establishing the school. Back in the primary stages of construction, we were having a difficult time because the managers at the government office were holding back their stamp of approval even though there was nothing wrong in our paperwork. The person in charge was very frustrated because of several vain efforts.

"It's just unbelievable. I go and ask which department's seal of approval we need, and still no department that I visit is willing to stamp out papers. At first, I assumed that there was something missing from our papers, but that wasn't it. I realized that there was an unofficial "rule". They needed bribes."

Among the many roadblocks that we've faced while preparing for the establishment of our school, this problem was particularly troublesome. We could clearly see the easy way out and it almost seemed foolish to stick to honesty. We really felt the temptation to compromise with reality. It would entirely be my fault if we were denied our construction permit because we didn't give any bribes, and I wouldn't be able to take responsibility for the lives of our faculty who had given up their good jobs for serving students at All Nations School. However, I decided to draw the Maginot line. We were not going to compromise even if it meant that we would be denied the construction permit.

The person in charge heard my decision, bit his lip, and replied.

"I will not be coming to school as of tomorrow."

My heart sank. However, his following words made we want to embrace the enormous man.

"I will go to the government office after breakfast every day. I will shove my face in their faces until they give us the stamp. I'll bother them until they do."

About a month later, I received a call.

"We got all thirty-three stamps! Finally!"

He told me that he- this man who was as big as an ox- burst into tears in front of all those people. He also said that the people at the office who were so uncooperative and derogative at first unanimously told him about the following on the day that he received the final stamp.

"When we first saw you, we thought that you were a high-spirited rookie who didn't know his way around things. However, as time passed by, we were moved by your truthfulness. Your school will definitely succeed."

This experience has made us more confident. That is 'honesty is the best policy'. As a Christian, the principle of my decision is Mattew 6:33, "Seek first the kingdom of God and his righteousness, and all these things will be given to you."

Honesty is the Best Policy

The most important value of education that we have upheld since the establishment of this school, is that lying cannot be tolerated. Lying leads to the destruction of character, mutual trust, and community. Just like how rubbish gathers in an unclean corner, lying will gather distrust and all kinds of nasty hearts. If we look at the records, all the students who had to leave our school had to leave not because of their wrongdoings but because of repeated lies. This is one principle that we will not compromise even if we are threatened by parents or at risk of slander.

Have you watched 'DocuPrime – The Private Life of our Child' that was aired by EBS, an educational broadcaster in Korea? This program shows an array of experiments on morality. For instance, they would make a verbal contract to give 100 dollars to people who participated in the interview with EBS. Then, they would give the interviewee an envelope on site and say, "150 dollars, right?" The experiment was to observe the reaction of each interviewee. Would they return 50 dollars or take the 150 dollars? Only 4 out of the 11 interviewees honestly returned the 50 dollars.

What is your image of 'honesty'? Do the honest lose? Is it okay to lie a little if it is to reach your goals? As much as most people emphasize the importance of honesty, not many are successful in living life with honesty. There is no reason for those people to choose to be honest when top scores and top salaries await them with just one closed eye. Thus, honesty falls far behind in people's rank of values.

In the same broadcast, Geum-Joo Gwak, professor of psychology at Seoul National University, also performed an experiment on honesty. She measured the level of honesty of 300 primary school students and selected the six highest scorers and six average scorers. The experiment went as follows. The children were blindfolded and were told to play a game of hitting the target. Everybody left the room, and the children were left alone with no watchers. Of course, there was a CCTV that was observing the children's actions. The experiment was to see how many children would complete the game without removing their blindfold.

What would you do if you were to do this experiment? Wouldn't you sneak a peek under the blindfold since nobody is watching? Six children had scored high on the honesty scale and the other six had scored just about average. The children who had scored high honesty on the honesty scale abided by the rules, but the children who scored average honesty either removed their blindfolds or moved closer to the target. Why did that do that? It was because we had promised to give them as many presents as the number of times they hit the target. The promise of more presents had made the children cover their conscience instead of their eyes. Prof. Gwak entered a series of experiments with several meaningful conclusions.

Honest children have the following qualities:
- High concentration
- Low aggression
- Better relationships with friends
- Low possibility of being bullied or being bullies
- High satisfaction in life
- Positive thinking that they can do it
- Strong belief in problem solving

After numerous experiments by many psychologists, they reached the common conclusion that 'self-control' is the key factor when it comes to cheating. What does it mean to have 'self-control'? It means that there is a higher possibility of self-directed lifestyle and studying. Children with high honesty actually achieved greater achievement in all aspects, including grades and social life, and experienced more happiness. Therefore, we can come to the following, precious conclusion regarding honesty.

"The more honest we are, the more competitive we are."

Joon's Honesty Training

Joon was a student with a wide range of skills. However, there was one thing that needed to be fixed. He had a habit of wanting to seem good in other people's eyes. He had fallen into the hypocrisy of wanting to 'seeming good' instead of actually 'being good'. However, Joon began to change through repeated honesty training. He then came before his friends to reveal his faults as well as his transformation.

Hello. My name is Joon. When I first came to this school, I realized that this wasn't an ordinary, easy school like the previous one. So, I decided to hide myself. I hid all my shortcomings, lack of skills, and mistakes from my teachers and friends. However, I realized after a long time that 'hiding did not solve anything. As time went by, I saw myself becoming a hypocrite who was different on the inside and out. So I began to reveal my weaknesses and flaws without being ashamed.

Today, I would like to share one of them with you. When I didn't have a phone card for international calling, I either memorized the card number of the person who was calling next to me or borrowed my friend's card, wrote the card number down, and used it whenever I needed to make a call. My actions were soon brought to light, and I felt so ashamed. However, that event made me realize what a two-faced person I was and gave me the momentum to change my ways. Now, I am no longer afraid of admitting my shortcomings and mistakes to make progress.

The thought that I want to share with you today is about being 'just the way you are'. 'Your friends, your teachers, and your creator all want to see the sincerity that is inside and not just the packaging.' 'Just the way you are' is something that can be applied in your studies as much as it can be applied to relationships.

Hesitating to ask a question because you are ashamed of your lack of knowledge will make you miss a chance to learn something you didn't know. If this happens repeatedly, it will become a boulder that detriments your growth. If you plan or do something without sincerity and just because you want to succeed and look good, your actions will only be an event in which you tried to look good and nothing more.

Additionally, I used to like showing off and standing in the spotlight. I was so ashamed when I realized that that was arrogance, but I told my shortcomings to my teacher and asked for help. Afterwards, the teacher helped me to change. I believe that everything starts with being 'just the way you are'.

Imagine what would happen if a smart and talented student like Joon grew up to be a hypocritical person. Imagine what a terrible influence he would assert on the future society. However, Joon has gotten rid of the façade of hypocrisy. Let's read the following letter to see how much he has changed. He has become a person of positivity and a challenge taker. Furthermore, he has become a passionate leader who encourages his friends and marches towards his vision.

"There is an old proverb 'to do despite knowing that it is impossible'. For example, humans have persistently attempted to fly despite knowing the obvious fact that we cannot fly. The attempt can seem stupid and can face mockery, criticism, or even persecution depending on the circumstance. It is all because the thought that it is impossible is planted deep down in everyone's hearts.

The world says that it is against logic and a foolish waste of life to attempt something that is impossible. Despite it all, I adore this proverb and aspire to follow it because our world is what it is today due to the people in the past generations who took on the challenge with a burning passion and continued to try the impossible. Humans cannot fly. It's true and it is impossible, but we now have planes that connect continent with continent all thanks to the people whose passion made the impossible possible. Seeing how we can achieve such impossible-seeming things, why should we give up before trying if there is even 1% of a chance?"

What is a successful education? It's not the admission rates into Ivy League universities or the number of alumni who become famous. If a student graduates without shedding their untruthfulness or hypocrisy and is admitted to a top university or becomes a famous person, there is a high chance that the education was a failure and not a success.

02

Moral Power is Developed Through Parental Love

Our school has a 'Reading King & Queen' policy. We gather all the book reviews that were written by our students and present awards once a month. Oddly though, the reward is a 'dinner coupon with the principal'. The Reading Kings & Queens who are selected each month get to go a fancy restaurant downtown and spend a fantastic time with the principal. This becomes a memory of a lifetime for the students because students cannot even dream of dining out with their principal.

The Reading Kings & Queens dinner with thachers

One day, Leah was chosen as Reading Queen. Leah had read the book 'Gasihi-Gogi(Stickleback Fish)' by Chang-In Cho, and she wrote a confession of love to her father after realizing the depth of his love through this book.

"The father stickleback fish protects the eggs in place of the mother stickleback fish that has abandoned her children and gone away. He raises them with care and then sticks his head amidst the rocks to die once his children leave his nest.
The protagonist, Daum's father in this novel is very much like the father of stickleback fish. He sells off the conscience and pride that he treasured the most as a poet to make money to take

care of his son who has leukemia. He manages to miraculously cure his son after selling his cornea but ends up sending Daum far, far away to France after he himself is diagnosed to be terminally ill. He yearns for his son until the last day that he dies alone at a mountain valley called Sarakgol, the place which stores his memories with Daum.

After reading this book, I cried my eyes out because Daum's father resembled our dad. Our dad, who sacrificed everything for his children and yet was sorry that he couldn't give us more....

Unlike some of my friends who feel a bit awkward around their parents, I am extremely close with my dad. We never even fought once. That was why I never thought that there was even a bit of negligence in our father-daughter relationship, and I was certain that my dad thought the same.

However, I learnt that this was my delusion when I overheard my father's conversation. My dad said, 'My children have grown so much that I feel kind of sad. I still remember the old days when the kids used to follow me everywhere' and made a sad smile. Only then did I realize how negligent my sister and I were to my dad after we each went off from home to study abroad and began to see a part of him that I hadn't seen before.

His black hair showed signs of whitening, his fingertips were stained with ink, and his old and worn-out shoes seemed so shabby next to my expensive new sneakers. I was shocked and heartbroken at this new side of my dad who had always seemed lively and confident. I was a poor daughter who was dissatisfied with what I had and took my father's abundant love and sacrifice for granted.

That's why I feel sorry and regretful for seeing the tired side of my dad only now. Also to think about it, the only reason that our father-daughter relationship was so great until now was all because of our dad's efforts. He had continued tat me and smile towards me even when he was tired and weary. It took me so long to realize that our relationship was what it was due to the endless efforts of our dad who invested all his free time in us even when he was worn out day after day of sleepless nights. I am sincerely grateful for my dad who always stands by me as a steady rock to rely on."

Finally, I want to take this chance to tell my dad that I got the courage to move on even amidst hardships because he was always next to me, that I will always remember his love wherever I am even after I become a full grown stickleback fish and leave the nest, and that I pray that he will live long and happily so that I may get the chance to return his love.

'I'm proud of you dad. I love you.'"

What would the father have felt when he read this paper? I'm a father too, and I can imagine just how happy Leah's father would have been when he received this letter. This is the fruit of education- to raise a child who respects their parents and is warm in heart.

Handwritten Letters that
Bridge Parent and Child

Gratitude and love towards one's parents along with honesty training act as a powerful tool that raises moral power. How can we raise the moral power of our students? Our school increases the moral power of parental love through the following method:

- Students write a letter to their parents every week.
- Parents also write a letter to their children.
- Students say to their parents, "I love you. Thank you."
- The school acts as a problem-solving intermediary for parent-child conflicts.

We need to teach our students to honor their parents if we want to raise their moral power. Humanity begins with honoring one's parents. It is the sad reality of our society that the beautiful tradition of 'honoring our parents' has changed into 'honoring our children'. We need to love our parents to honor them. We need to have a good relationship with our parents to love them. Then what can we do to improve the parent-child relationship? Is there a way to help both the parent and child simultaneously?

That's how we came up with writing letters. We got our students to hand write a letter (and not just email) to their parents every week. The results were beyond our expectations. Most parents told us that they cried tears when they received a letter from their children for the very first time, and we were able to observe relationships becoming stronger and restored.

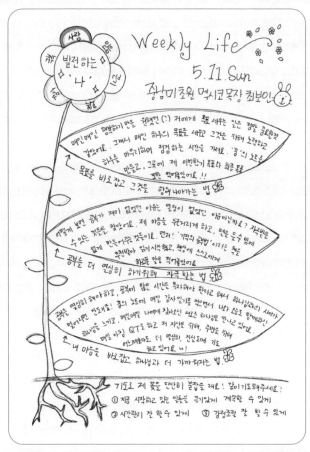

Weekly Life is a letter that students send to their parents for the past week.

Sonny exclaimed how his relationship with his parents had changed and shared the following story.

"My relationship with my parents really improved after I came to our school. Both my parents worked, and we had so little time to talk with each other since we only ate dinner together and spent the remainder of the day separately. We came across many quarrels and conflicts because we didn't know what each of us did. For instance, my mom and I would run into conflicts out of lack of understanding because my mom kept telling me to study and I would fight against her because I had my own plans.

At first, I thought that I would be better off here away from my parents. I had nothing but fun when I first arrived at school and got to live and study with my friends. However, I started to realize how much I needed my parents and began to feel thankful for them. My mom used to gather and do the laundry that I had left around the house, and she used to always clean my room. I finally learnt from experience as I did all those chores by myself here at school that she had raised me and taken care of me even though I was a brat and never listened to what she said.

I tell my parents, 'Thank you. I love you' whenever I call my parents. I didn't tell them that in the past, but I learnt to be thankful for all the little things as I experienced them firsthand. It feels like we have become a loving and caring family. I mean,

I'm always telling my dad that I love him when I used to be so awkward around him."

Parents also find it strange to write a letter to their children by hand. In many cases, letter writing leads parents to realize mistakes or emotions that they didn't understand before and to honestly ask for their child's understanding and forgiveness.

"Hey Mary~ Surprise!
There was a 'write a letter to your child' section in the book review, so I decided to write you a love letter from mom as a gift to you. I admit that I was a mom who was quicker to scold you than praise you, a mom who only pretended to trust you after saying that I would trust you, and a mom who was inattentive to your curiosity and attention.
I want to tell you once again that I'm sorry and that I'm thankful that you grew so well despite it all. You had to live under my strictness that was based on grades although you were a much warmer, understanding, considerate person than I and a kind daughter who made me proud. I was a mom who was worse than a stranger when I should have been encouraging you and trusting you. I'm sorry.
I am thankful that you are doing your best to change, and I am thankful to all the teachers who are staying by you. Dearest daughter~ Thank you for doing so well away from your parents,

and let's live every day in thankfulness. You will shine like a precious gem as you continue to try your best in your everyday life and as you steadily achieve your goals. Dearest daughter~ Mom will always cheer for you and pray for you. I love you."

How often are parents swallowed by the desire to make their children study? That is the source of conflict. Chasing after 'No. 1' incites competition. However, aiming to be the 'Only 1' is different. It allows us to acknowledge others in what they do well and appreciates ourselves for what we each do well. Friends are no longer competitors but cooperating companions.

On the day of parent visit, parents and children have time to bless each other.

03

Donation and Charity-
a Strength that Makes Miracles

A forty-year old judge said to a sixty-year old witness. "You've got to die if you're old." It is unbelievable that a judge, a person in a socially successful position, would say such words. This happened at a Korean court. What this judge lacks is moral power. Can we think of this judge as a great person just because of his job?

My country Korea has a particularly wide generation gap. Young people neither want to learn from nor want to stay close to their elders. Recently, the conflict between generations have peaked, leading to cases such as a vote among the younger people on whether to keep allowing senior citizens to have free metro transportation. How often do our teenagers interact with old people? Their encounters with the elderly are probably limited to visiting their grandparents on national holidays once or twice a year. An effective way to mature our children is to let them meet older people more often. They will learn humility as the thought crosses their mind that they will also grow old someday.

The population of Hope City, the city where our school is located, is ten million. There is a farming village near the downtown district, and there are many nursing homes since Hope City is a big city. The environment of the nursing homes is quite poor compared to those in other developed countries. Our school visits several nursing homes every week by dividing into groups. We prepare a few songs, dances, massages, and gifts for the grandmothers and grandfathers beforehand. Although communication isn't as smooth as we'd like due to the language barrier, this allows our children to learn how to communicate through the heart instead of words.

Time to talk with the elderly in a nursing home

Let me introduce Se-Rim's story after a volunteer visit to a nursing home.

"We visited a Nursing Home today. As we divided into our teams to learn some songs and dances and prepare with prayer, I became even more eager to leave a good impression and to make the elders laugh a lot. Although I had visited many nursing homes during the two years that I was at the school, I felt excited and happy as if this was the first time.
When we arrived at the nursing home, we saw old people lying on their own bed. They couldn't move freely, but they got up from their bed and shuffled to take a seat to spend time with us.

I fell in love with them who were overjoyed at our performances. We couldn't take our eyes off each other. I took the shoes off a old man's feet and gave him a foot rub like the woman who wiped Jesus' feet with her tears and long hair. I was doing it before I even realized it. His feet seemed so run-down unlike his kind facial expression. I massaged his cold, hard, and scarred feet with all my might.

I prayed that the warmth of my hands would melt his feet as well as his lonely heart. When it was time for us to leave, he couldn't let go of my hands as if he had opened his heart to me. It was very difficult to let go of his tightly grasping hands. He let go of my hands only after I promised that I would come back next time. I learnt and felt so many good things at this visit to the nursing home. We were able to share our love with them and receive their love in return.

It was such a thankful time during which we were able to bring joy to them by becoming their grandsons and daughters and valuable time in which we were able to share our love. I want to volunteer at this Nursing Home again to keep my promise with him."

Let Them Feel the Joy of Sharing

Our school has an audiovisual class period every Saturday morning where the entire student body gathers to watch a good program. One week, we showed our students 'Healing Camp – Aren't You Happy' by SBS, one of broadcasting companies in Korea.

During the program, Mr. In-Pyo Cha, a TV talent, wanted to share the story about how he wanted to share outwardly at first and how he changed from helping a few children out of self-comfort to helping with sincerity.

When Mr. Cha's wife was unable to go on a volunteer trip due to unforeseen circumstances, she requested him to go in her place, to which he unwillingly agreed. He was still unwillingly sitting in his business class seat when the rest of the team flew economy. However, he felt his heart move when he arrived at the destination and met a child. Although he should have been the first one to reach out since he was better off by all means, the child approached him first, reached out his hand, and told him that he loved him. The bright impression of this child who seemed to have no reason to be happy struck his heart and changed his outlook on life then and there. He then was introduced to one more person- pastor Jung-Ha Kim was determined to help the starving children but didn't have the funds. Pastor Kim couldn't stay still and suppress his burning passion towards the starving children, and so he began to shine shoes to fund seven children. Not long after, he was diagnosed with Lou Gehrig's disease which dried his muscles and drained his strength, making him weak and unable to work. When pastor Kim could no longer shine shoes, the customers who used to come to him continued his legacy to fund the starving children. It was a touching story.

The Miracle of Jung-Bin's Pocket Money

A few days after we showed this video to the children, Jung-Bin visited the principal's office and gave this letter to Principal Hyun.

"Dear teacher, Hello. I'm Jung-bin. Do you remember the video about actor In-pyo Cha that you saw at school? All through the video runtime, I kept thinking to myself, 'I want to devote myself and share the love too. Although I am studying abroad, I would love for there to be a way for me to help the children who are starving and suffering.' Around the same time, my sister asked me to pray for her as she went on a short-term volunteer trip to Cambodia. I prayed a lot for my sister and the Cambodian children. My sister had gone to teach English, and I envied my sister who got the chance to go and share the love directly through her body and words. During prayer, I kept getting the thought, 'Prayer is great, but I would love to help with my body, words, and possessions.' However, what could I do? I couldn't go further than just thinking because I couldn't drop out of school and fly to Africa.

During the principal's speech, he mentioned that our school helped many other places. Upon hearing this, I thought, 'Is there any way that I can help out? Is there a way for me to help others with what I have? I heard about that person who gave by saving up shoe-shining money. That's it! We need to abandon greed if we truly love someone, so I need to leave my greed behind and give what I prize the most', and when I sat down and thought about it, I realized that it was 'money' that I held most valuable. So, teacher, I ask you to use this money for a good cause. It's the pocket money that I received from my parents at Lunar New Year. I had never received any money larger than 100 dollars in my life, but I received a lot this time because I was older. I never had this much money before, and I took it with me to school because I was too scared to use it. Now that I am here, it is harder to come by a reason to spend it. I had stuffed this money deep inside my cabinet instead of putting it into my bank account, and it resembles the greed that has taken place in one corner of my heart.

I realized that I need to share this money. Would I even spend it well if I held onto it with my short thinking? I could purchase the electronic dictionary that I really need, but this time, I would like to spend the money for other people. I give this money to you, the principal, because I don't know anywhere that I can donate it to. I think you will use it for good. It's time for me to share the love that I have abundantly received, right?

The funny thing is, I feel so relieved and proud at the thought that I am abandoning my greed although I'm giving up a significant amount of money. Thank you for teaching me and helping me realize so many things and for loving me and challenging me to become a better person."

Principal Hyun was moved by the love in his student and suggested that we use this money the best way possible and create All Nations Foundations which our students could operate themselves. In the end, the 100 dollars that Jung-Bin donated became a miracle seed. A donation movement spread throughout the entire school like wildfire.

Mr. Cha's program reached Jung-Bin's heart and his offering became a spark that spread to 200 students. The money that the students collected for a year was a whopping 12,000 dollars. That was how the students established the All-Nations Foundation. The foundation investigates and helps regions all over the world. It began by affiliating with Compassion and is now giving help in numerous ways including supporting ten teenager head of households and ten primary students with financial difficulties, digging wells, and supporting orphanages in Myanmar, and providing prosthetic limbs in Kenya. Since this miracle was made possible through Jung-Bin's hidden pocket money, we call this the 'pocket money miracle'.

Kenyan children funded by All Nations Foundations

All Nations students with the primary school students funded by All Nations Foundations

A Warm-hearted Leader

It was World Aids Day, December 1st. A skinny, ten-year old lad called Austin Gutwein was dribbling the ball in front of the basketball hoop. There was a determined look in his eyes. His friends and family were watching him from the side with utter silence. Austin picked up the ball and took a free-throw stance. Then he flung the ball powerfully towards the net. His friends who had come to cheer him on swiftly caught the ball that fell to the ground and passed it back to him. One, two, fifty, a hundred…

Austin threw and threw. At first, he threw with unwavering power. Then as he continued to shoot, Austin's arms began to lose strength. He huffed and sweated, and yet continued to shoot with all his might. Why was he throwing the ball at the basket by himself?

The shoot count was now well over 1,000, then 1,500, and then 2,000. Austin's arms became numb and began to shake. His friends and family continued to cheer every time Austin made a shot. His body was now drenched with sweat. The number of shots Austin made at the goal that day was an incredible 2,057.

Do you know the story behind Austin's endeavor? Austin used to be an ordinary nine-year old kid who enjoyed watching animated movies and professional basketball. Then one day, Austin happened to watch a four-minute video clip made by World Vision. The story was about a Zambian girl named Maggie who had lost both her parents to Aids and was living in a dirt house. That short footage kept circling in Austin's head. Austin asked himself:

"How would my life be if that happened to me?"

After a lot of pondering, Austin got an idea from charity marathon events and decided to look for people who would donate a set amount for each free throw basket he made. On that day, Austin collected $3,000 which was passed on to eight orphans in Africa through World Vision.

Austin's touching story spread at his school. The following year, thousands of people including Austin's friends and neighbors collected donations by making shots. Austin's 'First Shooting' led to the miraculous donation collection of $610,000 in 2009 alone and that money was used to build dorms, clinic enters, and labs in Africa. There was an event in Korea called 'Shooting for Africa' through an international relief organization called 'Korea Food for the Hungry International(KFHI)' where donations were collected for poor children in Africa. The miracle that began from the free throw of a child (who is now a university student) has become a wave that sweeps throughout the world.

Shooting for Africa taking place in Jang Choong Gym, Seoul, Korea

Parents need to see Austin's influence and wake up. Many people these days think of volunteering as a part of 'fluffing up' the resume. What a sad life! We need to be able to see beyond the resume. Adults aren't the only people capable of great things. We don't need age or money to help someone. We shouldn't overlook what our teenagers can do. Children look for what they can do while adults look for a reason not to. Although we cannot change the entire world with what each of us have, we are perfectly capable of changing the world of one person. Our teenagers are no different from Austin. They can do amazing things.

Just as Austin Gutwein's 1-gram action created a miracle, we are also carrying out many donation projects. First, there is a jogathon called 'Run for Love.' The dorm members form a team and run around the playground happily. The second is a yard sale. As students grow, their clothes get smaller and are often thrown away. Because our school is a boarding school and we have students of all ages, we have a yard sale once a year. Faculty and staff also participate in the donation drive by purchasing clothing. The third is 'Birthday Donation'. It is common to receive gifts on birthdays, but at our school, students on their birthdays make donations. On special birthdays, students write thank you letters to their parents and experience the joy of giving rather than receiving through birthday donations. Also, instead of giving the friend a birthday present, the friends donate together in the name of the birthday student. All donated money goes to places in need around the world. Through these donation activities, students often say the following:

"As we run for love, we study for love."

Power Five

LEADERSHIP POWER

01

Self-Leadership

Self-Leadership Begins from the Binder

There is a book titled 'The Power of the Binder that Governs Outcome' by Gyu Hyung Kang. We revised this book for our use to make it more relevant to teenagers and call it the 'Growth Binder'. Our school helps students to manage themselves based on this book. We get the students to write a plan and vision for the first half of their lives or to write a Mission Statement and guide them to write out their plans in the order of short-term, mid-term, and long-term. Weekly plans are a must. We have to be 'professionals' who conquer time rather than 'slaves' who are dragged around by it. We can make progress when we compete with our past selves and not with other people. There is a saying which says, "'records' are our plans written on paper and 'plans' are the result of the recorded past'.

We utilize the binder to develop the thinking power of our students. Furthermore, the binder also enhances verbal expressive competency and builds life habits. We direct the students to record the following.

- Their dream, vision, and mission statement
- Monthly, weekly, and daily plans
- 21-day project to form good habits
- Living expenses management
- Reading management
- A record of their weekly life for their parents (letter form)
- Topics of gratitude and prayer
- All sorts of reviews (special lectures, travel, movies, etc.)

Yuri's Binder Story

"It didn't take long for the binder to become one of those things that every All Nations' student has. A binder refers to a type of notebook that has holes and an opening spring that allows us to move around paper without having to tear it. I can carry around any material from my teachers or letters from my friends easily by sticking them inside my binder without having to struggle with glue or tape.

Also, it is fun to decorate 'my own unique binder' that is different from the ones carried around by other students or teachers. We can make and fit a cover made of cloth or paper or decorate it with photographs or stickers. All the students decorate their binders uniquely as can be expected from teenagers, and each student's personality can be seen from their binders.

Utilizing a binder for a long period of time also leads to a habit of recording. We habitually pick up the pen, even just for a scribble since we always have a binder and pen near us. Although I initially wasted a lot of paper because I didn't know how to use a binder efficiently, I grew to record and store many essential things such as life plans, wise sayings, and pictures that give me motivation.

The binder makes it easy to store various records. I still have my report card from two years ago in my binder, and I often open it up for a moral boost of 'Alright! Let's try even harder!'

Our school also gives most of the certificates and letters from our friends in binder form. I'm thankful for that because it makes it so easy to store it in my binder. Last summer, I presented a binder to each of my parents because I wanted them to also learn about the usefulness of keeping a binder. Binders make a great present for anyone because it can be customized according to their personality. My parents now use their binders as a quiet time notebook and journal. Seeing how there are so many benefits to using a binder, there seems to be so many little things to be thankful for in this world."

Well-organized student binders. Students develop into professionals who conquer time through their binders.

Sunny's Self-Leadership,
A Change in Perspective

"My name is Sunny from grade 9 class 4. I experienced many changes during this semester. Among those changes, I would like to share with you how I've changed to become more active. Having a more active lifestyle doesn't necessarily only refer to seeming bright and active on the outside. It feels like my perspective towards everything has become positive, my grumbles have been replaced with gratefulness, and I've been filled with a renewed sense of love towards my friends and school once I decided to rejoice in everything and be happily obedient. Let me tell you how my perspective has changed.

First, my perspective has changed in my relationships with others. Although I seemed to others to be a bright student, I was timid and worried a lot. 'What's wrong with my personality?', Why can't I do it? Why can't I do my job? I was always full of thoughts of blaming myself. And because I lacked confidence, it was difficult to approach other friends first. It was through prayer that I was able to honestly let go of such thoughts, and slowly but steadily, I saw my heart become filled with thankfulness. Since then, I began to see others who were struggling and having a hard time, and I began to feel proud and rewarded whenever I approached to comfort them and share the joy that was within me. I realized that I became ever happier when I shared my light with other people and picked them up. Now I am so happy that I can stand alongside so many people.

Second, my perspective has changed in all the school activities that I participate in such as choir activity, class activity, and Ranch activity. When I was assigned as singer team leader and class décor leader this semester, I was filled with thoughts like, 'Why did I become the leader when there are so many other students who are better than me?' and only wanted to avoid the role. However, I went on to honestly open to my friends about how burdened I felt and received their help, and this changed my perspective from 'What if I make a mistake? What if people thought I was strange? What if they hate me?' to 'I'm happy that I am able to put a smile on their faces.' To the surprise of many people, I was able to make people smile with even more confidence as my perspective changed for the better.

Third, my perspective has changed in my relationships with my teachers. As many of my friends already mentioned, there are so many great teachers at our school. However, I used to find it difficult to approach them when I lacked confidence because I was afraid that they would figure out my weaknesses. However, the love and kindness they gave me changed me 180 degrees. Now, I approach them more often to talk with them. I grew to love my teachers so much that I went from worrying 'What if my answer is wrong?' To share my answer with confidence even if I was wrong, my teachers tell me that they like how active I am and encourage me to grow even further."

There was a reason why Sunny has transformed into an amazing student who always has a bright complexion. It was because of her attitude change. She had changed from negative to positive, from grumble to grateful, from passive to active, from timid to confident, and from caring towards herself to care towards her friends. As such, self-leadership requires a taste of change in attitude. Schools need to help students reset to a positive mindset.

Sam's Self-Leadership, Love for Oneself

"How satisfied are you with who you are right now? I'm satisfied, not a full 100%, but about 99%. I still wish that I was a bit better looking, better at sports, or better at singing, but this wistfulness is only 1% of my life.

I was able to learn 'how to love myself'-something that I didn't know about back in the past- thanks to our school that taught me to think positively and to be thankful. Instead of being hurt by what other people say about me, I look back at myself, improve what I lack, and move on.

Sometimes when my friends complained about how we don't have an air conditioner, I ran over to a sweet spot in front of the fan to cool my sweat and study. Also, when some people pointed to me and said, "We can't win against him because he is a genius", I picked up my pencil and studied even harder during my free time to become the person that they saw in me. I didn't sway at any complaints of boredom about our repetitive daily routine and lived a joyful life by finding something new every day. When everybody else was having a hard time focusing on their studies, I tried to have conversations with our teachers by offering to carry their books.

I couldn't live such a life due to my own merits. I believe it was all made possible because I learnt how to love myself through the lessons which taught me to think positively and to be thankful in everything. Although I still have a long way to go, I want to live a meaningful life because God loves and treasures me.

As such, I am continuing to learn how to live with joy at the school. Whenever I see my weakness, I encourage myself with a cheery, 'I can do it!' and focus on my potential instead of pressurizing myself. This attitude has changed me from being the timid person that I used to be in the past into a bright and active person."

That was a great explanation by Sam about his transformed self. Isn't this the joy of education? It is rewarding to see a child change from being passive to active and pessimistic to optimistic and to watch them transform from being a self-centered brat to a considerate friend and from being a restless squirmer to a genius student. What does it mean to 'love oneself'? It is to only care about oneself. We often find ourselves being particularly merciless towards ourselves. We get scared, unsure whether we can do something right because we see our weaknesses and how we fall short of others. We need to learn how to praise ourselves at times. We need to know how to embrace ourselves as is. We need to encourage ourselves, saying, 'You did well. Great job. You will continue to do a good job tomorrow'. This is not pride. It is only those who know how to love themselves that know how to love others. People who do not know how to love themselves only ask for love and do not think about loving others. People who love themselves can find things to be thankful for even in the middle of uncomfortable circumstances. They have the composure to find potential in an impossible environment.

A person with self-leadership is bound to assert influence on their community. Thus, there is a high chance that they will become the leader of that community. For such people, we need to enhance their group leadership.

02

Community Leadership

Joy's Room Leader Leadership

I'd like to introduce this essay by Joy. This essay made me realize that taking on the position as room leader is the best leadership course available. As important as the role of a room leader is in the dormitory, students often show tremendous growth in leadership after they assume the position of room leader.

"I was appointed as room leader for the very first time this semester. I learnt and experienced so many things as I took on the position. The room leader is an important position that can directly influence the room members (: room family). So, the first thing I learnt was the responsibility of leading my room family. Although I didn't have to take care of extremely small details since I shared a room with only current students and no newcomers, I felt the need to take extra care to guide and support them since they knew and thought that much more about the school.

Secondly, I learnt that I had to be a good example for my room family. I can still see how the actions of each of my previous room leaders have influenced me. Actions speak much louder than words. Therefore, it is much more helpful to show through example rather than only by words. This benefited me too because I got to look back at my own life whenever I pointed out a room member's mistake.

Thirdly, I learnt about communication. If there was one thing that made our room different from the rest, it was that we told each other a lot of things. We would talk about so many things including petty comments like, "You look better in this color, and for you, this one!" We were able to approach each other more sincerely through such conversations and were able to learn more about ourselves through the eyes and comments of our room family.

Finally, I learnt that I had to show even my weaknesses to the younger students. I used to absolutely hate showing my weaknesses to the younger students. However, I had no choice but to draw upon my experiences when talking with someone who was struggling with their problems. When I told the students, "I had many weaknesses too, but I was able to change to become the person that I am today", they regained strength from my experience and tried to change. Additionally, they were able to approach me with more sincerity because I opened my weaknesses to them. Thus, we were able to grow even closer. I experienced the joy of transformation through Jane, learned to not be bound by my emotions through Lora, and learned willpower through Dana."

Hee-Jin's Vice-Shepherd Leadership

"I believe that All Nations School is a place where a 'family community' is truly realized among all the nations. We are still young teenagers who are yet to grow even more. It isn't easy for people of our age to leave our families, our old school, and the society in which we used to receive recognition and to resettle in a new place.

I am thankful for the attention and care that I received from my Ranch when I was a new student and recognize how subtly helpful it had been. I learnt a lot from my classes and leadership as well as from my new lifestyle. That is why I believe that the Ranches play an important role. Ranches become another family for us and become a new type of love.

Vice-shepherds play an important role too since Ranches are of such great importance. Vice-shepherds shouldn't be arrogant and should be the first to serve. They should approach and serve their friends first. I hope to go beyond collecting the 'weekly life' every week and announcing the meeting location- I will listen to the concerns that our members have and take a step further to provide guidance or insight to help them solve the problem or grow from the experience."

This essay was a letter of declaration written by Hee-Jin after she became a vice-shepherd. The vice-shepherd plays an extremely important role alongside the shepherd teacher of the Ranch. Being appointed as vice-shepherd means that their leadership is acknowledged by everyone. After undergoing leadership training for smaller groups of four to six members as room leaders, vice-shepherds become the effective leader of a Ranch group of about twelve members. The most important leadership training at our school takes place through the room leader and vice-shepherd experience because it is like practicing being the mom or dad for the members. Therefore, the role of the vice-shepherd is crucial. That is why we have the vice-shepherds reflect upon themselves through the following checklist every week:

- Check if my life set an example for others
- Have Quiet Time so that I will be centered correctly
- To first be a good follower (of teachers and officers)
- To encourage and have conversations with my Ranch family every day

- Engage in deep conversation with my Ranch family at least once a week.
- Check if anybody is being left out and to spend time with them.
- Meet with the shepherd teacher twice a week
- Serve and love with sincerity without being two-faced.
- Be willing to help Ranch families who ask for help.
- Pray for my Ranch friends
- Collect and submit weekly life reports and reviews on time.
- Encourage book reports

Hee-Jin's Vice-Shepherd Checklist

Name: Hee-Jin   **Date:** 11/25~12/1

Item	Check	Details
Check if my life set an example for others	–	Others say that it's enough but there's still room for improvement.
Have Quiet Time so that I will be centered correctly	V	Psalms 2
To first be a good follower (of teachers and officers)	V	I followed with thankfulness.
To encourage and have conversations with my Ranch family every day	V	I greeted everyone I met with joy. Received encouragement.
Engage in deep conversation with my Ranch family at least once a week	V	I slept out with my Ranch members and spoke with them individually.
Check if anybody is being left out and to spend time with them	–	Nobody was isolated (in any way)
Meet with the shepherd teacher twice a week	V	Weekly, pocket money, sleep out plans, etc
Serve and love with sincerity without being two-faced	V	I'm not sure about serving. But there were no two-faced moments.
Be willing to help Ranch families who ask for help.	V	We helped each other
Pray for my Ranch friends	V	Thinking of each person
Collect and submit weekly life reports and reviews on time	V	
Encourage book reports	V	I was encouraged instead

Anybody Can be a Leader.

Who is a leader? Our school teaches that 'a leader is a person who asserts a good influence on their friends anywhere including in the sports field, dormitory, Ranch, and extracurricular activity group. Leadership isn't the sole property of those who have a special skill or record. The key is how and to what extent they can have a good influence on their community with what they have.

While there are numerous books that claim to help enhance leadership, it is impossible to demonstrate leadership without experiencing it hands-on. The students at our school learn about leadership through their lives. Then, they read a book on leadership every week and either write a book review or prepare a seminar. This helps them to systematically organize everything that they have experienced.

Sung-Hoon entered Beijing University. This essay that he wrote while reminiscing about his life at All Nations School may provide the best explanation on community leadership training.

"The 'leadership' that I learnt during the few years that I was at All Nations School has matured me and overturned my way of thinking and living completely. I came to study abroad at this school when I was only fourteen years old. The one thing that I saw, heard, felt, and experienced here from a very young age was 'leadership'. While I didn't quite know or understand what leadership was when I was still young, I naturally became interested in what a leader was and what their role entailed as I grew older, and I also got the chance to learn about it firsthand as I accrued various experiences in school.

Leadership is an influence. A leader is an influential person who leads others to go towards a vision and goal together. I became attracted to this fascinating topic of 'leadership', and seeing my interest, my teachers taught me what it meant to be a true leader and showed it to me by setting an example. They taught me everything: the wisdom to distinguish what is right to lead to the proper path, how to serve from behind rather than to ruthlessly pull from the front, the gentle leadership that raises people, and the steadfast heart that is grateful in every situation and unwavering in the face of hardship.

Our school taught us the proper mindset and actions through community life at our dorms, Ranch gatherings, autonomically operated foundation, student council and provided us with the opportunity and environment where anybody, and not just the few students who were good at it, could be a leader.

Once I became a highschooler, I gained so many valuable and meaningful experiences as I served as a student council officer. Hosting the council meeting, planning the nursing home visits, staging school events, and counseling the younger students....All through middle and high school, I learned and trained through these leadership lessons that cannot be learned elsewhere. It was a time during which my leadership capacity was amplified through in-depth analysis and thinking on leadership.

Later, I led the leadership enhancement project for the junior students where I shared all the know-hows, the proper character that leaders should have, and the most important factor of leadership- trust- that I had learnt through my first-hand experience. It was a great time through which we were able to grow together.

I still have a long way to go as a leader. However, I have great expectations for the future- one in which I will have become a true leader who asserts a good influence on the world and write history as the light and salt of the world."

03

Social
Leadership

Outreach, An Intensive Course to Social Leadership

Every summer, our school sends students to teach English at primary schools nearby. That is the Outreach of our school. Our students learn and feel many things by going outside for various activities during the Outreach period. I eagerly await the Outreach each summer because what we learn through this time cannot be easily learnt or gained from any other place.

Although our students teach for only about a week, the preparation process begins a week earlier. First, we organize groups. The entire student body is divided into about twelve groups and a leader, and two vice-leaders are appointed for each group. Students who aren't closely acquainted can end up in the same group since students from all grades are mixed. The awkwardness in the beginning slowly changes into unity and students learn to understand each other in the process.

Once the groups are decided, we gather into our groups to share our resolutions and mental attitude. Then we pray together in preparation for the Outreach. Our title of prayer was to be able to pass on all the love that we have received with the people that we will meet. Afterwards, we formally begin to prepare the lessons. We gather ideas on what we will teach each day, how we will teach, and what activities we will incorporate. Then we divide each group again into four teams of three so that each team can be responsible for a day of class.

At the most recent Outreach, I belonged to a team that was responsible for Wednesday. The three younger students in our team and I decided upon a theme for our lesson and made the preparations. Since our theme was 'Exercise', we gathered a few balls (like basketballs) and prepared a PowerPoint presentation. We prepared some songs and games too. We were filled with uncertainty and anticipation throughout the preparation period. I felt nervous although it was my fourth Outreach because I had always only helped the elder students and had never taken the lead. I also felt resentful and thought, 'Why aren't there any older students in our group?' However, I was able to lead the lesson preparation till the end thanks to the students around me who encouraged me each time that I felt pressured and tense. The lesson slowly revealed its outline as we continued to hold meetings and lesson preparations for three days.

Then it was finally simulation day. I couldn't talk or laugh because I was so tense. The simulation was a complete mess. Furthermore, I really felt like crying and giving up because even the presentation skipped or got stuck. I still remember the desperation and heavyheartedness that I felt back then. I felt incompetent and felt terribly sorry for the younger students who had followed me. Just as I was about to burst into tears, the group leader called me over for a talk. He told me that I was already doing great and encouraged me so that I could regain the strength to continue the preparations. I still feel grateful to him. I really needed the encouragement that I was already doing a good job.

We prepared with even more effort after we messed up the simulation. Finally, we randomly picked the names of the children who we were to teach. During Outreach, each of the students randomly selects a child to pray for and to pay special attention to and care for. The child that I had picked was a boy called Tienxi. I prayed that this child would come tomorrow with his heart wide open although I didn't even know his face.

A photograph of the yearly Outreach. Students spend time singing with and teaching English to the children of a primary school in the countryside.

We met the children on the following day. As on every Outreach, I thought the children were very cute. The smiles on the children's faces make me feel happy. However, they didn't show us their beautiful smiles because it was the first day. So, we decided to do some ice breaking. We introduced ourselves, took pictures together, and made name tags. I felt so thankful for the children who were participating more actively than I had expected. Thankfully too, the child whom I had picked had come to school that day. He was so cute! He grumbled every time I said let's do this, or let's do that, but he participated most wholeheartedly. I had to run a lot because the child ran around quite a bit, and he laughed whenever I was out of breath. We slowly grew closer.

The children replied and laughed out aloud even during the lesson that continued after the ice breaking activities. The 4th class period flew past as we played games and danced. We felt sad when the class had to end but we said our goodbyes, and promised to meet again on the next day, had lunch, and had a meeting time with our groups. We were all exhausted at the meeting although we had rested for an hour before gathering. We hadn't realized it while we were playing with the children, but we were completely worn out and tired because of all the playing, running, and piggybacking.

However, we prayed for new strength and prepared the lesson for the next day. It was lunch time, preparation time, then dinner time before we knew it. That was basically the gist of the three days.

We grew close with the children during those few days and the children opened their hearts to us. It was a physically daunting but a truly joyful time.

The final day arrived just as we were getting used to being together. We tucked in our sorry hearts and picked up the camera. We also packed the candy bracelets that we had prepared and greeted the children at the door. We felt a sadness that was unlike the previous days. We tried to stay with the children as much as possible and took more pictures together.

The final event was a talent show by the children of each team. The children put on face paint and performed the dance and song that they had learned in our classes. Our team drew a red heart on our cheeks and performed a dance on stage. I was able to see all the children since I was dancing in front of the audience. I felt delighted to see them dance enthusiastically. The children seemed so lovely, and I truly felt sorry that it was time to say goodbye. After the talent show, the children's parents came to pick up their children. We couldn't hide our sadness when we parted. I teared up when we hugged tightly and promised to meet again. The End! Our group met up for one last meeting, wrote our reviews, and shared what we had felt. Although I had expected to feel as free as a bird at the end because I was quite concerned and pressured at first despite the awesomeness of it all, I felt a sadness, bitterness, and emptiness in my heart. The time of sharing was filled with thankfulness and God's presence. It was a time of truly valuable learning. Outreach was a tiring and yet joyful time because God was with us and a memory that I wouldn't exchange for anything in the world. I am grateful that we were able to go out and share the love. I love Outreach. I am already excited for the next one although it is far from now.

This Outreach review by Jina is so vivid, that I can almost picture all the activities happening before my very eyes. This is the Outreach program that is held by our school every year. Students take the week that comes between the end of spring semester and beginning of summer vacation to visit a primary school in the countryside and teach English. Preparations begin a week earlier. The students spend the week creating a daily schedule, curriculum, and textbook. Each team assigns members to teach singing, lead games.... It really is a big challenge. Students are required to speak instantly in both English and Chinese and the facilities of a countryside school are something they need to make do with. Restrooms are in a corner of the sports field and infested with flies and maggots. Our teachers put their beloved students into these difficult environments where they need to solve everything by themselves. Children are given obstacles to overcome without giving up. Rather than continuing to struggle, difficulties are given to them so that they can triumph.

The reviews of the children who have returned from Outreach make me think that they have learnt so much more than they would've gotten from mere words or books. They become parents and call the children their sons and daughters. They become teachers and understand the hearts of their own teachers. They understand the importance of communication by speaking in both English and Chinese. Students begin to study even when they are told not to once, they return from Outreach. They also become kind. Let me share a few of the reviews by the students.

"I learnt the heart of our teachers by teaching at Outreach. I thought about what and how I had to teach to facilitate the children's learning, paid attention to the emotions and state of each and every student and supplemented their weaknesses- and these were just a few of the many things I had to pour my care into. I learnt just how much effort our teachers had to put in for us."

"I learnt about the preciousness of studying as I was teaching the students. I realized that I had to know a lot to deliver the knowledge effectively. From now on, I will try my best in everything, including studying. I'm sorry that I troubled the teachers so much until now."

"I want to experience more change. I learnt a valuable lesson that we can do anything when we come together. I would like us to be even more unified at the next Outreach so that we can share more love with the children and experience more personal growth."

"I learnt that I need to open my heart and approach the children first in order to be welcomed by them."

"I became more confident in my English and Chinese language skills through this Outreach. It wasn't easy to teach English in Chinese, but I confirmed that it was possible."

Growth of Global Leadership Through Chinese and English

In order to prepare the G2 era, we came up with the Sino-American Program (SAP) to prepare students for studying in the United States. Now it became a study program where we catch Europe, Australia, Canada, and Singapore as well as China and the United States. Students participating in SAP not only master the Chinese language but also study through a systematic English curriculum and a U.S. middle to high school curriculum before going even further to attempt the AP Program. At the same time, the system organically combines a variety of extracurricular activities and social service with the goal of multicultural global servant leaders. At present, the SAP is made up of students from all over the world such as Korea, USA, Australia, Singapore, Hong Kong, South America, etc.

SAP students say that they can feel their understanding and outlook on the world broaden. Let's look at the students' reviews.

"I really think that All Nations School is the only school where get to utilize three languages as we attend Chinese class with our Chinese friends, go to SAP class to talk only in English with our foreign teachers, and chat in Korean with our friends." (Minhee)

"Learning three languages simultaneously allows us to compare the three languages and learn two things when we are taught one. I want to become a person who is able to utilize all three languages of Korean, Chinese, and English to move people's hearts and have a large sphere of influence. My dream is to become an international lawyer. I want to be able to solve large international problems, help foreign workers in difficult situations, and defend the human rights of people with disabilities. I believe that fluent command of several languages is the key to change the world and influence people." (Lynn)

"I used to only speak English because I was born in the U.S., but I learnt Korean and Chinese also after coming to this school. Learning a language goes beyond simply learning grammar. I love how it teaches me the cultural background and widens my perspective." (Erin)

Erin added a fine conclusion to her thought. Her words made me proud that he was studying the languages with a clear purpose and not just for another line in her resume or for the prospect of a higher future salary.

"Knowing different languages can save lives because it can be the bridge between two different countries."

For example, Underwood came to Korea at the end of the Chosun Dynasty as a missionary and established a college, the predecessor of Yonsei University. Do you know what one of his greatest achievements was? First, he passionately studied the Korean language. Then he published the Korean-English, English-Korean dictionary in 1890. This was the very first English dictionary in Korea. It allowed many Koreans to learn English with ease and allowed many other foreigners to learn Korean through this bridge.

What kind of leadership should 21st century leadership be? Firstly, it should be multicultural. In other words, it should be an encompassing leadership that understands different cultures. Secondly, it must be global. Even though the means of transportation and communication were not developed in the first century, Jesus told his disciples to go to all nations, to baptize them, and to make disciples. He had a global perspective that he would not be done right now, but his teaching would be realized globally with the development of civilization. Thirdly, it must be servant leadership. Have you heard about the servant paradox? You will be uplifted when you humble yourself, and others will uplift you instead of you doing it for yourself. This is the leadership that we should aspire to. We call such a leader a Multicultural Global Servant Leader. This is the goal towards which we are nurturing young talent. This is the reason why the school should be more than a place where we accrue knowledge, it should become a power station- a 'Powernasium'- where we can raise our good power.

Power Six

BODY
POWER

01

Brain Wearing
Sneakers

'Zeroth hour PE' has recently become a thing. The term 'zeroth hour PE' was first used by Dr. John Ratey, Clinical Professor of Psychiatry at Harvard Medical School as the title of the first chapter of his book 'Spark Your Brain'. The book introduces the effects of the 'zeroth hour PE' experiment that took place at Naperville Central High School, Illinois, U.S.A. The freshmen were told to run 1.6km in the sports field at zeroth hour period with a heart rate monitor attached to them. After a semester passed, the students who participated in 'zeroth hour PE' showed a 17% increase in sentence comprehension since the beginning of the semester and received grades that were twice as high as those of the students who didn't participate.

Professor Ratey's book reverses the stereotypes trapped in our minds. In the past, schools were worried that PE classes would drain the child's energy for studying, but it does not have to do this. As broadcasted by KBS News, one high school in Seoul was already putting zeroth hour PE into practice.

> "First period class is somewhat.... blurry...in the head. But my head becomes incredibly clear after I exercise."
>
> – Woo-Jae Kim (Second Year, Goohyun High School)

This school made a class of students exercise before regular classes for two months and the results were astonishing. According to the teacher's ratings on the students' lifestyle such as class concentration, students who exercised scored an average of +6.2 on activeness whereas students who didn't scored -1.9. Furthermore, eight out of ten students who exercised in the morning showed an increase in their first semester mid-term grades, with the increase in math grades being much greater than students who didn't exercise. This experiment reaffirmed the long-standing truth that studying requires stamina.

The Brain Science of Exercise

Our school has been practicing 'zeroth hour PE' since it was established in 2003. The entire student body wakes up at 6:00am and gathers in the sporting field. Then we jog together for 30 minutes. This program was started, not for the purpose of waking up, but to wake up our brains. In addition to this, we have many body power programs to wake up students' brains:

- Get up in the morning and jog for 30 minutes.
- Continue the 10-10(10:10AM) exercise(stretches and jogging) for 30 minutes.
- The entire student body does Taekwondo.
- One of the three extracurricular activities on Saturday should be a sport.
- The entire student body goes ice staking in the winter.
- Hold a school-wide inter-class basketball league.
- Perform a basic fitness test every semester to enhance physical strength.
- Learn sports dance and encourage girls to play badminton.

Professor Ratey said that the function of the frontal cortex, which is responsible for memory and thinking, improves when we sit and study in front of a desk but is also similarly activated through exercise. In other words, the thinking part of the brain is not that different from the exercising portion. Furthermore, exercise develops the entire brain equally since it facilitates the growth and division of brain nerve cells and the production of BNDF(Brain Derived Neurotrophic Factor) which allows the smooth passage of signals. BNDF can be seen as a sort of nutrient fertilizer that can aid in the production and growth of brain cells. Fun fact: it has been discovered that aerobic exercise can cause an increase in BNDF concentration. These are scientific secrets that have been uncovered since the 90s. Ultimately, exercising makes you smarter.

The book 'Brain Development Learning Method' by Professor Nagae Seiji introduces a study on the relationship between running and memory by Professor Gubotabo Kisou from a social service university in Japan. He analyzed the difference in short term memory between people who went running 2~3 times a week and those who didn't. The short-term memory for both groups before running was around 65%. However, the test that took place twelve weeks later revealed that the score of the group that went running had increased to 95% whereas the score of the group that didn't stop at 70%.

Aerobic exercise such as running and jogging increases the cardiopulmonary function of our body. The heart sends 5 liters of blood per minute under normal circumstances and 50 liters per minute of cerebral blood flow during aerobic exercise(which is ten times the normal rate). Thus, much more oxygen and nutrients reach the brain and facilitate brain activity. Exercise creates new blood vessels in the brain and increases the volume of capillaries whereby increasing brain function alongside blood flow to the brain.

Professor Ratey emphasized the immense effect of exercise on the brain. First, it develops a healthy mental environment and increases concentration. Second, it promotes the production of neurotransmitters that are suitable for studying which expand neural circuits which in turn prepares the brain to receive new information on a cellular level. Third, it speeds up a stem cell developing into a new nerve cell inside the hippocampus. To summarize the mechanism of how exercise effects the brain:

"Exercise → heart rate increases → cerebral blood flow increases → oxygen and nutrient supply to the brain increases → brain cells are activated → learning capabilities including memory and concentration increases → grade increases."

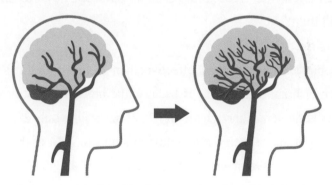

Increase in cerebral blood flow is connected to enhanced brain function

The document program 'The Future of School PE' by EBS, an educational broadcast in Korea, shows how the school in Naperville schedules important classes after PE class. For instance, a student who is falling behind in math is scheduled so that their math class would come right after PE class. Then the student's concentration would increase during math class. This is because exercise causes the number of brain cells to increase which causes the amount of information that the brain can process to increase. However, new cells disappear quickly if they are left unattended. The cell requires ample stimulation to survive in the brain and be used as part of a new system that processes information, and placing a difficult class immediately after PE class serves to stimulate the brain cells that have been created through exercise. Zientarski and Lawler who began the 'zeroth hour PE' project in Naperville said,

"The PE teachers create brain cells. It's up to the other teachers to fill them."

Aerobic exercise is more effective than weight training for the purpose of brain health. This is because the brain lives with oxygen and dies without it. Although the weight of the brain is only 2% of total body weight, its oxygen consumption amounts to 20% of the body's total. What does this mean? Professor Castelli of Illinois University, U.S.A., studied 259 primary school students to observe the learning ability of the students who showed either high or low levels of oxygen consumption. The result revealed that children who had high levels of oxygen consumption studied better than those who had lower levels of oxygen consumption. Aerobic exercise triggers the production of nerve growth factor in the brain. This stimulates the neurons to branch out even more and tightens the connection between neurons. In other words, it strengthens the network between brain nerve cells and increases the information processing speed.

Do you want to be smarter? Then run. Brain power comes from your feet. Your brain will tire out if you only sit and study. Exercising before studying makes your brain cells healthier, whereby making new neural circuits flourish in the brain. This makes your brain smarter.

Connect PE Class to Brain Development

We utilize a portion of the benefits of PE class. Instead of teaching our students how to play a game of sports, we focus on teaching them how to maintain their health. It's because this is connected to the healthy life of the students. Let's summarize why exercising is crucial for teenage students.

First, it helps them to overcome stress. Teenagers these days are maxed out with academic stress. When their brain burns out, it triggers feelings of anxiety and tension which leads to an increased production of cortisol. Exercise removes the excess cortisol that was produced due to chronic stress.

Second, it makes life more enjoyable. It has been proven through multiple studies that exercise is more effective than antidepressants. Exercise increases the connection between serotonins, BDNFs, and neurons whereby relaxing the hippocampus that had shriveled up due to depression or anxiety. Restoration of happiness leads to the improvement of overall living attitude and makes it easier to maintain social relationships or make new relationships with other people.

Third, it increases the desire to study. Exercising causes lowered levels of dopamine, the core neurotransmitter related to desire, to be restored. Dopamine enhances the connection between neurons whereby desire automatically increases along with grades.

02

The Ability to
Control Food Intake

- High consumption of carbonated drinks
- High consumption of fast foods (e.g. hamburgers)
- Low intake of vegetables
- Skipping breakfast often
- Irregular meal schedule
- Picky eating habits

This list is a summary of the eating habit trends of teenagers. Check your eating habits or your child's eating habits on this list. How many points did you check off? According to the 2013 Report of the Korea Centers for Disease Control and Prevention, one out of four teenagers drunk carbonated sodas at least three times a week. More than one in four teenagers skip breakfast at least five times a week. 1.3 out of 10 teenagers ate fast foods such as hamburgers or pizzas at least three times a week, and only 1.6 out of 10 teenagers ate vegetables at least three times a day. What results can we expect from such eating habits in our teenagers?

Grades are Influenced by Breakfast

The Rural Development Administration of Korea performed a study on university freshmen and sophomore students in 2002. The topic of the study? The relationship between breakfast and college entrance exam scores. The results showed that students who ate breakfast everyday scored 20 points higher on average than students who had breakfast less than five times a week. Their score was 10 points higher than those who replied that they had breakfast 5~6 times a week and 13 points high than students who had breakfast 3~4 times a week. Thus, their college entrance exam scores increased with the frequency of breakfast meals.

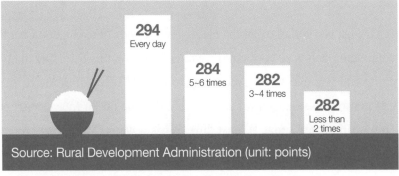

294 Every day

284 5~6 times

282 3~4 times

282 Less than 2 times

Source: Rural Development Administration (unit: points)

The Relationship Between Breakfast and College Entrance Exam Results

Students studying for college entrance exams, and parents of such students, are clearly aware just how much of a difference can be made by one to two points. Students are often rejected from their dream majors because of a single point, so how significant of a difference would 13 points be? The same results can be seen from school grades. Students who eat breakfast more regularly received better grades in school.

A similar study took place in Japan. Among freshmen students in junior high school, students who ate breakfast everyday scored 62.7% on the five major subjects whereas students who didn't scored 57.1%.

What do these results reveal? They reveal that breakfast influences brain activity. Glucose is the energy source of the brain. The brain uses 5g of glucose per hour. However, the brain doesn't produce or store glucose- it is the liver that stores glucose in the form of glycogen and then breaks it back into glucose whenever it is needed. However, the liver can only store up to 60g of glycogen. Thus, the brain can supply the brain with glucose for up to 12 hours. If we have dinner at 7:00pm and do not snack until the next day, we can assume that the brain will have a supply of glucose until 7:00am. Then we need to have breakfast by least 7:00am because at that point, we will have run out of the glucose that the liver can supply to the brain. Imagine going to school without having breakfast in this situation. The brain will have to hibernate. It is foolish to expect high levels of concentration in such a circumstance. Also, it is unrealistic to dream of getting good grades.

Chewing food properly also plays a role in activating the brain. Chewing thoroughly has more benefits than just easing digestion. There was an experiment with two mice. One mouse was given only hard food, and the other mouse was given powdered food. Intelligence tests showed that the intelligence level of the mouse that ate solid food was higher.

At our school, all our students enjoy their breakfast because we wake up at 6:00am to jog and shower. Their eyes sparkle wide with the energy supplied and blood vessels expanded leading to the brain. That is why we have no students dozing off in the morning. Their concentration and perseverance have heightened because their brains have received plenty of energy and oxygen.

The Strength to Control Guts

What is a 'meal'? We can call the process of food entering our body (including the brain) through our mouths and integrating with all our cells a 'meal'. Then should we eat only the food that we enjoy eating or food that our blood vessels and brain like to eat? The answer is quite simple. Stuffing our bodies with instant food, fast food, and all kinds of meat for the pleasure of our mouths is food thrown away.

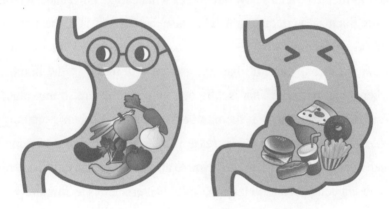

Healthy stomach, healthy brain

There are 100 trillion bacteria living in our body. The total weight of bacteria amounts to 1~1.5kg which is roughly the weight of our liver. Most of the bacteria live in our intestines. Intestinal bacteria include beneficial, neutral, and harmful bacteria. What would happen if we continued to feast only on food that harmful bacteria enjoy? The beneficial bacteria will starve while the harmful bacteria will be happy and multiplying daily. Therefore, eating only meat and almost no vegetables is like paying dues to harmful bacteria. There is even a joke that says that even cannibals would not eat the 'modern man'.

If harmful bacteria dominate the intestine, it brings with it phenomena such as obesity, constipation, atopy, irritable bowel syndrome, and rancid gas. Harmful bacteria feast on proteins and fats whereas beneficial bacteria survive on carbohydrates and fiber. The two have completely different eating habits. That is why what goes into our mouths decides how our bodies will change. Intestinal bacteria do not fluctuate in number much because there is a limit to the amount of food we are able to ingest as well as space. Therefore, an increase in the number of harmful bacteria causes a decrease in the number of beneficial bacteria. That is why our eating habits are so important. Wouldn't it be fantastic if the number of beneficial bacteria naturally increased to counteract the increase in number of harmful bacteria? Then again, we cannot use medicine to annihilate the harmful bacteria because a controlled amount of harmful bacteria gives us immunity.

The recent surge in atopic dermatitis has been named 'atopy (unknown and odd)' because we did not know its cause. Atopic dermatitis doesn't get better through dermatologic treatment. However, its cause was recently discovered. Atopy is caused by a broken balance of the immune system. Then what caused the balance of the immune system to break? A drop in beneficial intestinal bacteria and activation of harmful bacteria had caused the production and absorption of necessary vitamins, mineral, and amino acids to drop. We need to increase the number of beneficial intestinal bacteria to maintain a balanced and healthy ecosystem in our intestines. There are two ways to do this. We could consume the beneficial bacteria directly or control our eating habits to increase the beneficial bacteria in our systems. In other words, we can consume a lot of vegetables and fermented food products such as kimchi that are abundant in beneficial bacteria. Beneficial bacteria dismantle the food that enters our intestines and aids in the absorption of nutrients into the bloodstream. Consequentially, vitamins, hormones, and enzymes are produced, metabolic activities are facilitated, and cells are activated in our bodies.

Intestinal Health is Brain Health

Professor Michael Gershon is the author of 'The Second Brain' and a professor of pathology and cell biology at Columbia University. He is also known as the father of neurogastroenterology. There are 100 meters of nervous system that runs along our digestive system from our esophagus to our anus. Professor Gershon discovered that a neurotransmitter called serotonin plays a crucial role in the enteric nervous system. Furthermore, he continued to study the interrelation between the enteric nervous system and the medicine or food that we ingest.

His research teaches us that our intestines serve more than for just a digestive purpose, they actually affect our emotions and actions by secreting neurotransmitters through the nerve cells. We can think and act positively when our intestines are healthy, but we can become depressed and even develop behavioral disorders if we have too many harmful bacteria and too little beneficial bacteria in our intestines.

Our intestines and brain influence each other. Intestinal health greatly influences our mental health and mental health greatly influences intestinal health. Gershon revealed that 95% of our serotonin is produced in our intestines, as the beneficial intestinal bacteria helps in the synthesis of serotonin. If we have insufficient levels of serotonin, we find it difficult to control our emotions, feel depressed and irritated, and become more aggressive. It can be said that a large part of our emotions is influenced by the nerve action from our intestines. The enteric nervous system uses over 30 neurotransmitters just like the brain.

To summarize, food not only influences our bodies but also our minds. Therefore, the happiness or unhappiness of our lives can be decided by our good eating habits in the following way.

"Good food → increases beneficial bacteria → increase in physical well-being and mental positivity → we become smarter and live longer."

"Bad food → increases harmful bacteria → breaks our immune system and makes us mentally unstable → triggers all sort of physical illnesses and mental disorders."

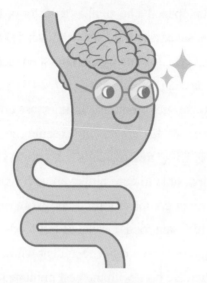

The Second Brain: Our Intestine. Our intestine is connected to the brain.

Love Yourself Through Your Eating Habits

Have you heard about the book 'Disease-Proof Your Child' by Joel Fuhrman? Fuhrman had hurt his leg while he was a figure skater. The doctor prescribed that the leg needed to be amputated. However, Fuhrman refused to receive the surgery and chose to fast. One year later, Fuhrman competed in the 1976 Figure Skating Championships that took place in Spain and won bronze medal. Everybody was surprised. Since then, he had a newfound interest in the effects of food on the body and went on to study at the University of Pennsylvania School of Medicine. Fuhrman's study was focused on nutrition and immunity.

Post graduation, he opened a hospital as a doctor of Family Medicine and achieved great success as a doctor with over 5,000 people visiting him during the first year. Fuhrman didn't insist on medicine or surgery. He stuck with improving eating habits.

Fuhrman introduces how food has an immense effect on children's brains by referring to his treatment experiences. Eleven-year-old George Grant was an aggressive child who always came last to his school. It was impossible to cure him even with sedatives. The mom came to Dr. Fuhrman completely tired and worn out. Fuhrman kept George on a diet of 'brain food' instead of fast foods for three months. The result? George became a diligent student who even came first in his school. Children are born with the best immune system created by God. However, prospects are dim if we keep eating foods that harmful bacteria like and that starve the brain. It isn't hard to see what will happen to the children if we look at the eating habits of the parents. Parents who enjoy junk food raise children who enjoy junk food.

It is necessary to raise food management strength in our children. People who excel in controlling their diet also excel in their studies. Why is it so? The answer lies in the frontal lobe. People with developed frontal lobes are good at studying and good food develops the frontal lobe. In conclusion, excellent diet control leads to front lobe development which leads to excellent self-control. Excellent self-control leads to enhanced self-leadership such as time management. This is called the 'positive cycle of food'.

Food Management Strength Increases Brain Competitively

What do you think it means to be good at your studies? Do you think you'll be able to study well if you stay up all night? Then that's as if you are saying, "I am stupid". We need to prepare the optimum conditions for the brain to study. Why? Because it is the brain that does the studying. In this case, we'll need to supply the brain with enough energy to move, make the intestines comfortable enough so that it will make the brain happy, and increase the blood flow to the brain. Then, stimulate the brain in that optimized state. You will experience new knowledge being sucked up into your brain.

We have observed the wrong eating habits of teenagers today and studied how proper nutrient intake has a huge impact on learning capability as well as on general well-being. Do you want to do what you really want in the future? Then stay away from the junk foods that please your mouth. Controlling your food intake is another kind of strength. Increase your body power by managing healthy eating habit. This will increase your brain power.

Power Seven

———

SPIRITUAL POWER

———

01 Learn about Death
02 Learn about Life

01

Learn
about Death

Remember Death

This audiovisual lesson was a meaningful time for me. I thought about death, wrote my will, and made a resolution to try hard and live like there is no tomorrow. Dear mom and dad, try setting apart some time to think about your death. I was filled with emotions of sorrow and gratefulness as I wrote my will. I couldn't stop crying."(Sooah Cho)

I watched the program 'Last Words, Remembering Death' by SBS with our students. This video was a great production which got us to think about a new meaning of life through people who left a will in the face of death or prepared a will assuming death, as well as through the thoughts of people who had experienced the boundary between life and death.

After we watched the video, we took some time to look squarely at the matter of our own deaths by assuming that we were each about to die soon. Then we wrote our wills. At first, the students seemed to care little about this topic as they hadn't thought about it before. However, they began to sniffle and wipe tears away as they wrote their wills following the screening of the video. There was a solemn air to the classroom with one child here wiping away a tear, one child there thinking with their eyes closed, and another few children scribbling away with their pens. Even the students who liked to chatter remained silent in this moment.

We take death class seriously here at All Nations School. The death class at our school is carried out in the following order.

- Watch a program or video which will get students to think about death carefully.
- Write a will.
- Experience being trapped in a coffin.
- Visit a hospice ward.
- Read a book that lets the student face the reality of death.

Ryan's Will

"To think that I would write a will...I really didn't expect this day to come for me. Mom, dad, Justin, I'm sorry. I'm also really thankful and incredibly proud that my family was stuck by my side, that my mom was my mom, that dad was my dad, and that Justin was my little brother. Looking back right now, there seems to be nothing remaining. I wonder what I lived for, and regret postponing things when I was going to die like this anyways. The fact that I regret the most is that I had lived a selfish life where I didn't share what I had or loved other people. What is the meaning of having a lot of things in this world when it will end up as nothing once I die? Why didn't I share when I could have saved a life by sharing the love? Why was I so busy filling my own stomach? They say that people on their deathbeds are only reminded of the times that they helped others. Those were the greatest times…so why didn't I see where true happiness lies?"

Yuna's Coffin Experience

"Last week, we experienced death with our Ranch friends. I was scared and filled with all kinds of thoughts at first because I heard rumors that we were going to go into coffins and that we had to wear dark clothes. My friends and I whispered, "Are we actually about to die?" as we went to the leadership center. When we went in, we became even more scared because everybody was wearing black as if they were at a funeral. I learnt something new as we learnt about death. One message that came home to my heart was that death was living again. I was afraid of dying from a young age and I was so terrified about death that I would jump into a fright when I saw anyone die. However, I became slightly relieved when I heard that dying was being born again in heaven. As we learnt about death, each of us tried getting into an actual coffin. Honestly speaking, I was really surprised.

Never had I ever imagined myself getting into a coffin. Sure, I may have imagined it once or twice when I was watching TV a long time ago, but I didn't know that it was going to happen like this. Still, I think it is a really good experience. Everything became quiet and dark when I got inside the coffin. My emotions changed from scared to comfortable to somewhat nice once I settled in. Students outside began to cry as we each stepped into the coffin. I started to cry too because I suddenly remembered my family. There was no stopping the tears. I began to think more and realize more things during this time. First and foremost, I felt thankful that the people I loved were still with me and so thankful for my loving and caring parents."

Students look back at their lives and reset the values and purpose of their lives through the coffin experience.

Learn about Death

Dostoevsky was sentenced to death at the age of twenty-eight and was given a final five minutes in his cell to look back on his life. Thankfully, his sentence was cancelled just as he was about to be executed. Later on, he remembered the five minutes before execution and lived every day with thanks, as if each was his last, and went on to write masterpieces such as 'Crime and Punishment', 'The Brothers Karamazov' and 'White Nights'.

It is an important lesson to 'perceive death'. Spiritual Power is the strength that allows us to look at life and death properly. Perception of death has the following benefits to the children.

- It helps them to establish their attitude, self-identity, and values.
- It helps them to realize the sanctity of life and get away from the isolation, sadness, and sense of loss.
- Students reflect upon their relationship with their family.
- They look back at their relationships with those around them.
- They start living life to the fullest at the thought of death and gain love for others.

Education on death has taken place widely and internationally since the mid-20s. In the United States, the course 'Dying and Death' was first opened at the University of Minnesota in the 1960s. In 1976, the Association for Death Education and Counseling(EDEC) was established to raise experts on death education. The curriculum of death education at school includes reading books about death, visiting funerals and cemeteries, and watching movies or pictures on the topic for discussions.

In Japan, death preparation education was first introduced in 1966 by Takahashi Makoto who was a social studies teacher at Geio High School. At first, he received criticism from the students and parents that it wasn't appropriate to teach about death to growing children. However, he persuaded them that studying well mustn't be the only goal of life and that students would be able to reach specific life goals and directions by studying about death. As the effects of the lessons exceeded the expected benefits, death education eventually became a core course of Geio High School and was introduced to schools throughout the country.

Our country is also starting to become more accepting towards death education. Some non-religiously affiliated universities registered a course on death. Previously, schools that opened death education classes for teenagers have mostly been religiously affiliated schools.

Not the End, but Completion

Why do we have to learn about death? Why do we have to face death? People intentionally escape having to think about death. Thinking about it makes us afraid and depressed because we think that death is the end. However, isn't there another word that depicts death more accurately than the word 'end'? Death is the 'completion' of life.

"It is finished."

These were Jesus' last words on the cross. Even as He was being crucified, Jesus didn't say 'my life has come to an end' but that 'everything has been finished'. Although the final breath had escaped His physical body, His life had finally been 'completed'. Completion! What a heart pounding word! It is as if we've become artists of our own lives. Don't you feel like pouring out your efforts to create the most beautiful painting? This is why we need to be educated about death.

Our students didn't write anything in their wills like, 'I wanted to get into an Ivy League school' or 'I wanted to earn a lot of money and go anywhere and eat everything that I desired'. Rather, they wrote about how they regret hurting their parents and living like they would live forever. Their wills are filled with words like, 'I'm sorry. Thank you. I love you.' One of the students wrote the following phrase that rang in my heart.

"I realize that only love lasts forever in the face of death. I may be leaving, but I am leaving my love with my mom, dad, brother, and friends."

All the students realize at the face of death that a valuable life should come before any qualifications or money in the priorities of life. They realize that we shouldn't be wasting our lives. They realized that life is meaningful and precious. Our lives are valuable because we only live once and we are valuable because there is Only 1 of us. Whatever your view on the afterlife may be, you are precious because you are the Only 1 and your life lasts Only Once.

Bronnie Ware was an Australian woman who worked as a bank clerk before she moved to England with the determination to find her true dreams. She ended up helping many old people who were on the verge of death, and all the old people told her what they regretted the most in their lives. The regrets were summarized into five main points which she published under the title 'The Top Five Regrets of the Dying'. The book became an instant bestseller. The first regret that the book introduces is not being honest to oneself and living the life that other people desired for them to live and living to show instead of living according to one's own dreams. The book states that to live according to others' expectations or to live to look good in others' eyes is a 'fake life'. It's a life that chickened out from living a 'true life'. In other words, it was a life stuck in the competition of survival like that of a hamster stuck on a wheel. It was a confession of regret towards a life that had not gone out to search for true value.

We become spiritual when we face the identity of death. Our lives become filled with true spiritual power. How do the following sayings reach your heart? Share it with your children and discuss your opinions.

"Unless a kernel of wheat falls to the ground and dies, it remains only a single seed. But if it dies, it produces many seeds."(The Bible)

"Death is a change of the outer shell that covers our soul. Do not confuse the shell with what is within."(Tolstoy)

"We do not care about our being while we ignore death. Being aware about death becomes the way of life that allows us to face our potential."(Heidegger)

02

Learn
about Life

Storage Life vs. Pathway Life

A miser cried with remorse at his death bed.

"I only taught my children about money, the value of money and how to earn money…but what does all that mean at the end of life?"

None of us can be free from such regret. We tell our children to have a 'dream beyond a dream'. The first dream can be a dream job. Many people aspire to have a stable job, a high-paying job, or a boast-worthy job. These are dreams that are visible. We will leave words of remorse like the miser above if we end with just this. We can call this life a 'storage life'. Its meaning? - A life that only tries to fill.

We need to have a 'dream beyond a dream' if we want to go beyond a storage life. We need a dream that sees far, thinks of the future, and aspires to a value that cannot be seen. People who have this do not give up on life easily. This is why our teenagers need to have a 'dream beyond a dream'.

Let's look at an example. There are two people who hope to be primary school teachers. One person is motivated by comfort, stability, and good pay whereas the other envisions a life of a tree-planter and hopes to help each student to grow into a good tree. If the first person is chasing after a dream that can be seen, the latter person is going beyond such compensation and chasing after a value that cannot be seen. The latter is living a 'pathway life' that goes beyond 'storage life' where they can pass on their blessings to those who are in need. Such aspirations arise from spiritual power and our society needs individuals who are equipped with that power.

Kristal's Pathway Life

I would like to introduce someone to you. She is a graduate of our school and currently a junior in university. We received a letter from her a few days ago. She explained that she had received a scholarship and that she wanted to donate the money to All Nations Foundations because it was the first time that she had earned money. This is her letter.

"Hi, I'm Krystal and I am an alumnus of All Nations School. It's still cold there, isn't it? Hope City has the most spectacular winter that can be seen from nowhere else. After finishing my finals, I decided to stay in Beijing to do some stuff. I was able to find a good job, so I'll be teaching Korean to Chinese university students and doing some translating. Enclosed is the first scholarship that I've ever received. I give it to All Nations Foundations with the desire to offer all my first fruit to God. I feel so joyful with not a speck of regret.

I received so so so much more wisdom when I studied with the thought that studying was a form of worship that I can offer as a student. I remembered that it was the school that had taught me that 'studying is a form of worship' as I was looking for the right place to donate my scholarship.

Dear teachers! I would like to take this opportunity to thank you once again for teaching me the true reason to study. Thank you for guiding me away from goals like earning money, meeting a nice guy, or getting married. Thank you for guiding me to study with hope and faith unlike other people who study against their will. I feel so grateful to have gone to the school and received a great education."

It's as if Krystal's heart is literally made of crystal. If I were me, I would've wanted to get a new smart phone or iPad to enjoy myself. It is easy to see that a student like her will lighten up the world. I remember receiving a question a long time ago from a person that I respected.

"Will you be someone who feeds 5,000 people or a person who eats

5,000 people's worth?"

There is another movement happening. 38 students have decided to establish a school for the future generation. One teacher who was moved by their determination offered 10,000 dollars that was in their bank account as seed money for the school. These students have decided upon and have begun preparing towards a good dream and vision in this busy and selfish world. Their lives are the definition of a pathway life.

"A Second All Nations School will be established soon or later. We don't yet know where and how, but we are already prepared in our hearts. We anticipate that this school will be completed by our hands and with the wisdom and love we have received at our school. I want to meet heart to heart with the many children who will come to our school, spend sleepless nights to support their dreams, and pray with tears for their sake. I want to do as the teachers at our school do. I have truly received so much love from my teachers and I want to share this love with our students.

One day, my parents came to me after they had dropped by our school for parent's visit day and told me that our teachers looked so happy. This would have been unimaginable in other schools. The teachers have a much harder time than regular teachers. They must stay up all night at our dorms, memorize the names and details of every single student, stay at school during vacations for the sake of the students who didn't go home...but most of all, they have to put in so much effort and sacrifice in order to care for and take responsibility of the children who are studying abroad and away from home. (I am always in awe when I think of our teachers.)

Still, our teachers are happy. While I cannot fully grasp where that happiness comes from and what it feels like, I can understand that it is the most prized thing of all. That is why I want to feel that happiness myself someday."

Self-denial First, Then Self-fulfillment

There is a message that I emphasize to the students.

"Discard your dreams. It's an empty dream.'

People say that we need to hold on to our dreams, but we teach our children to abandon them. Why do we do this? We can figure out why if we peer closely into each of our dreams. Most dreams arise from each person's selfish desires. There's a whole bunch that also comes from the brainwashing of the parents. The great majority of dreams aspire to an abundant and pleasurable life for oneself. That's why we teach differently from the rest of the world. 'Discard all the dreams that are for your own survival and success.'

If we look closely at what people aspire to, we can see that their aspirations are the same essence and just different in form, teenagers and adults alike. Students worry about getting better grades and adults worry about getting promoted. What's the difference between the two?

While it is of course important to encourage self-fulfillment, self-denial must come first. Self-fulfillment without self-denial is like building a house on sand. A house can be strong and steady when it is built on rock. If we think about it, Jesus came to this world to enable us to live even more successful lives.

"Then he called the crowd to him along with his disciples and said: 'Whoever wants to be my disciple must deny themselves and take up their cross and follow me.'" (Mark 8:34)

"Whoever finds their life will lose it, and whoever loses their life for my sake will find it." (Matthew 10:39)

Why did Jesus come to us? We are unable to achieve true self-denial and instead only desire our own selfish success because we focus too much on the 'God bless you' part. This turned Christianity into a religion with ups and downs.

We must truly experience meeting Jesus. The confession 'I have been crucified with Christ' of Galatians 2:20 is much more earnest when it comes from the lips of teenage children. Sometimes children can be more spiritual than adults.

"I have been crucified with Christ and I no longer live, but Christ lives in me. The life I now live in the body, I live by faith in the Son of God, who loved me and gave himself for me." (Galatians 2:20)

We need to undergo the complete death of our ego, experience a life unified with Christ, and then pray for a true vision so that we may be used as a pathway by God. As such, our dreams have already been decided as Christians. Look at the following Bible verse.

'But you will receive power when the Holy Spirit comes on you; and you will be my witnesses in Jerusalem, and in all Judea and Samaria, and to the ends of the earth.' (Acts 1:8)

Our dreams are without a doubt to become 'witnesses'. Being a witness has a different meaning from being a missionary. We cannot, and should not, raise all our graduates as missionaries. To be a witness means that the person exerts a good influence through their lives and that they are used to saving people. Therefore, the purpose of studying should be to save people and not for one's own success. Based on this definition, a job cannot become a dream. Jobs are merely tools used to achieve a dream. Thus, we should not set a job as our vision. Even today, there are many adults who limit their children's dreams to the world. That's why they can't break out of the boundaries of the world.

"You are the light of the world. A town built on a hill cannot be hidden." (Matthew 5:14)

Search for the Right Place to Die

C.S. Lewis said in his book 'Mere Christianity':

"Christ says 'Give me all. I don't want so much of your time and so much of your money and so much of your work: I want You. I have not come to torment your natural self, but to kill it. No half-measures are any good. I don't want to cut off a branch here and a branch there, I want to have the whole tree down.'"

What do many people who claim to be Christians and those who claim to preach the gospel these days emphasize? 'Jesus came to save us?' Well, this is correct too, but that's not the entire reason that Jesus came to this world. I teach our students that 'Jesus came to kill us.' Then the students ask a question.

"What do you mean? Jesus came to kill us? Didn't he come to save us? I've never heard about this before!"

Eunice drew a comic as a review after hearing this sermon and made the following confession.

"I won't live like a zombie that is neither dead nor alive. I will die with my Christ at the cross, come back to life, and live as one with God's heart."

What do you think? We must die completely in the hands of Jesus. It is through this experience of death that we can live in righteousness and in God. My partners and I are devoting our lives to raising such disciples.

> "He himself bore our sins" in his body on the cross, so that we might die to sins and live for righteousness; "by his wounds you have been healed." (1 Peter 2:24)

In the meantime, I was having dinner with my colleague teachers who came from the United States. As we had some tea after the meal, they mentioned that they had a prayer request and told me the following.

"We are looking for a place to die, not to live."
"What? A place to die?"
"That's correct. We used to live in Hawaii, a place that some may call the best place to live in this world. However, we believe that the right thing to do is to look for a place to die, not to live."

It felt like I had been hit in the head with a hammer when I heard this statement. Jesus came to this world to die for us. Therefore, as

Christians, we should be looking for a place to die rather than a place to live. However, these days everybody is busy looking for a 'place to live'. We move to better educational districts, move to places where the house prices are expected to jump...it's almost as if the motive of our lives is to 'Move to a better place to live!'

As they said, perhaps the proper attitude towards life for Christians is to search for the 'place to die'. Of course, this doesn't mean that we must absolutely move to desolate environments. However, we must have a mission to focus our lives on, wherever we may be located.

'This is how we know what love is: Jesus Christ laid down his life for us. And we ought to lay down our lives for our brothers and sisters.' (1 John 3:16)

Are you searching for a place to live or a place to die? Do you live for your selfish interests or for a mission? I pray that all the students that I teach at All Nations School will find a vision to drive their lives and a place to die for that mission. I pray that they will find the place to offer, not just so much, but their all to God.

One of our graduates, Sonia, sent us a letter at the start of this year. She shared her resolution to stand with the teachers of the next generation and wrote about the empowering experience she had had during her life in university.

"As I think of 'Seven Power Education' of All Nations School I graduated from, I could feel the numerous attempts that were made and heaves of effort that was poured into the students by the teachers. After graduating high school and coming to university, I was finally able to see the tears and prayers that had melted into everything that I had taken casually thinking, 'It's part of my education'. The definition that 'studying is process of raising power to exert a good influence' gave me a greater sense of mission. I would like to share how I raised my seven powers during my four years at university.

First, network power. While most people text to ask how somebody is doing, I always tried to be the first one to make a visit. It was because I had learnt that we should look into a person's eyes and talk to them face to face if we wanted to have a conversation. That may have been why I found texting to be frustrating. So I decided to create an activity called Pin-Chan(where we went to the school cafeteria and sat in front of a friend that we didn't know. We would share our lives with that friend while dining together) during campus meetings which eventually allowed me to make many international friends. Since I learned and made it a habit that the first step in human relationships is face-to-face and heart-to-heart exchange, I was more accustomed to looking at people's faces than looking at my smartphone.

Second, mental power. One of the comments that I heard the most from those around me while I was in university was 'I'm jealous of your positivity'. I also used to be a complainer. I was once a grumbler because I complained so much about all the friends who were better than me, all the assignments, and all the classes that were difficult to understand. However, I knew about the immense power of positivity because I had already experienced it when I was in All Nations School. Therefore, I decided to make a gratitude tree in my home. The legacy of the gratitude tree had followed me to university. Everyone who lived in or visited our home proceeded to fill the gratitude tree with gratitude fruits and soon the abundance of the gratitude tree translated into abundant gratitude in my life. My life began with gratitude just like the Bible verse, 'Give thanks in all circumstances!' and soon became a bundle of gratefulness that led others around me to also become people who could give thanks.

Third, brain power. my friends and I still gather today to study together. We would study in our respective universities and gather to study together and share help if anyone was having a hard time with math or language. A friend who is good at math always makes time to teach math to the other friends. I also received help from a friend who is good in Mandarin when I was struggling in the language course. We do this because we already know the joys of growing together and the truth is that knowledge becomes tenfold when it is shared. Additionally, we share what we have studied and other materials in politics, economics, and more whenever we hold our campus meetings so that we may grow together as brilliant minds.

Fourth, moral power. there are many Korean students studying abroad at university who zuòbì, or cheat. Everybody cheats a little because there are many courses that require memorization, and it's really hard to dismiss the temptation. One day, my friend Brian who is attending Fudan University in Shanghai gathered the courage to go to the vice president of the university and tell him what was going on because he thought that it wasn't right to cheat during exams. Brian faced a bit of oppression from the senior students but didn't get into too much trouble. A few days later, more instructors were positioned in the study abroad exam to monitor cheating and this eventually led to good fruit. Brian had shown me how one ounce of action is worth a ton of theory'. We are continuing to try hard and implement walking the honest path.

Fifth, leadership power. I am currently living outside of school with three younger students. I tend to have more free time than them since I am attending the second semester of my fourth year. So, after thinking of all the ways in which I may serve the younger students, I began to spend my mornings washing the dishes, doing the laundry, and cleaning the house. I always admired and wanted to gain leadership that serves from behind, so I feel like the happiest person now that I get to implement it and put it to action. The younger students began to serve me during the weekends once I served them first. It seems like I've led them by serving them.

Sixth, body power. Everyone at our home drinks detox juice once a day. Also, we also made an assignment for the community within our home and that is to exercise 30 minutes every day. We are committed to maintaining our physical strength because we know that a bright mind and a good heart, however great they may be, will amount to nothing without physical strength to back them up. We are trying to live healthy lives to serve as many people as possible.

Seventh, spiritual power. 'How can I give glory to God' is the question that is first and foremost in my mind when I make decisions for my future. It is because the purpose of my life isn't to achieve satisfaction and success but to bring Him joy. 'Will

I be the person who feeds five thousand people or someone who eats five thousand people's worth alone?' I will be a person who feeds five thousand people even if it means that I myself won't get to eat. I'm filled with joy and happiness just at the thought of it. I won't be afraid when I stand before death later on; instead, I will be cheering with joy at the fact that I'll finally get to meet my God. I look towards my death with anticipation. "The good shepherd lays down his life for the sheep."
I still live exerting the influence that I've learned at All Nations. Now I hope to become a shepherd who teaches it."

Sonia's confession that she hopes to become a shepherd warmed my heart. This is the time when biblically powered leaders are needed as the uncertainty of the future grows as the 4th industrial revolution era unfolds. We as educators should offer the proper path to this generation. My fellow teachers and I will continue to go against the world and stick to the leader-nurturing principles that God truly desires instead of following the trends of the world because we know that God's principles on education will always overflow with power through generation to generation until His day comes.

HOLISTIC POWERNASIUM
BEYOND SCHOOL

초판 1쇄 발행 | 2024년 9월 6일

지 은 이 | 최하진

펴 낸 이 | 윤성
펴 낸 곳 | 나무&가지
북디자인 | 김한희
마 케 팅 | 임지수
등록번호 | 제 2017-000048호
주　　소 | 서울시 서초구 강남대로 455, A동 511호
편 집 부 | **전화** 02-532-9578
이 메 일 | sevenpoweredu@gmail.com

ISBN 979-11-91366-04-4 03230

이 도서의 국립중앙도서관 출판시도서목록(CIP)은 e-CIP페이지(http://www.nl.go.kr/ecip)
와 국가자료공동목록시스템(http://www.nl.go.kr/kolisnet)에서 이용하실 수 있습니다.